Harden's

London for Free

Sponsored by **Mercury one2one**

© Harden's Guides, 1994

ISBN 1-873721-06-4

British Library Cataloguing-in-Publication data:
a catalogue record for this book is available from
the British Library.

Printed and bound in Finland by
Werner Söderström Osakeyhtiö.

LRT Registered User No. 94/2126

Harden's Guides
PO Box 1500
London SW5 0DX

Contents

The mobile phone • For everyday • For everyone

Harden's London for Free guide and Mercury *one2one* are ideal companions for an enjoyable, inexpensive and hassle-free day out in London.

With a *one2one* phone at hand you can check the opening hours of places you want to visit and if you are having a good time and stay longer than planned, a quick call home puts everyone in the picture. Mercury *one2one* is a phone for people not places, so no matter where you are, you are never more than a phone call away.

For everyone

Mobile phones are fast becoming an everyday part of life for people in all walks of life – not just in business – and in their short ten year history, their popularity has outweighed all expectation. Soon after the first mobile appeared in the UK in 1985, it was predicted that there could be as many as 50,000 in use by the end of the 'eighties. The prediction was wrong by a factor of 20. Today, there are over 2.7 million mobile phone subscribers in the UK, with numbers growing daily.

In 1993, Mercury *one2one* turned the telecoms world on its head when it launched its service in London and the South East offering customers free off-peak local calls – a first for the industry. In the days following the launch, the company received literally thousands of enquiries from interested people and after just one year, has over 140,000 customers. Gone is the "yuppie" image of the 'eighties as the mobile phone moves out of the board room and firmly into the hands of the family. So far, around two-thirds of *one2one* customers are new to mobile technology, having never used a mobile phone regularly before.

Why buy a mobile phone?

Just like the washing machine, dish washer and microwave oven, the mobile phone adds extra freedom and control to busy lives, so there is more time to get on with the things that matter. Whether at home, work, or out and about, Mercury *one2one* lets you keep in touch at all times. It is easier to organise a busy schedule, keep up with friends and family and have fun.

Cost is no longer an issue with Mercury *one2one*'s competitively priced call charges, so you can use the phone to share a joke, have a moan or simply to catch up with the gossip knowing the bill will not break the bank.

There are many built in features and services which are all part of the standard package when you buy a

Mercury *one2one* mobile phone. For example, VoiceMail, which acts like an answer machine, greeting callers with your own personal message. If you're in a restaurant or just don't want to be disturbed, simply switch off your *one2one* and collect your calls when it's convenient. To help you stay in control of costs, *one2one* provides a fully itemised bill and you can choose to bar calls to overseas and premium rate numbers. It's up to you.

With the best value for money tariffs in its service area, including free off-peak local calls, making good use of your Mercury *one2one* mobile phone won't break the bank.

Friends and family will pay less to stay in touch with you on your *one2one* too, as whichever price plan you choose, it costs between 50% and 60% less to call from a conventional telephone to a *one2one* phone than it does to call some other mobile phones.

What can I expect from the Mercury *one2one* service?

While no mobile phone can guarantee perfect calls every single time, digital phones such as Mercury *one2one* can offer a vast improvement in reliability over earlier types of mobile phone. Because it is a digital system, eavesdroppers can no longer listen in to calls and a stolen *one2one* phone can be black-listed, making it worthless to criminals.

Another major difference between Mercury *one2one* and the old fashioned mobiles is the SmartCard. The key to your *one2one* service, it stores your personal mobile phone number, holds a record of the services you have chosen to complement the *one2one* standard service package and even stores up to 99 names and numbers in your personalised "phone book." Every SmartCard owner will receive their own bill; this means that a *one2one* phone can be shared by members of a family, or a business, each with their own personal SmartCard, allowing them to choose the services which best suit their individual telephone needs.

A growing network

Mercury *one2one* is available not just in London, but across the South East and in Birmingham and the West Midlands, reaching 30% of the UK population. With a steadily growing network, the service is on target to cover the country by the end of the decade.

The Mercury name has long been associated with choice and value and Mercury *one2one* now brings these qualities to the mobile phone. The first phone which is truly affordable, Mercury *one2one* is the mobile phone for everyday for everyone.

For Details on Mercury *one2one* FreeCall 0500 500 121

The mobile phone • For everyday • For everyone

The mobile phone • For everyday • For everyone

Introduction

What can you do in London for free?

World-famous parks, beautiful ancient woodlands, great museums, spectacular annual events and superb entertainments – London has an unmatched range of free attractions.

In fact, the great thing about London is that many of its very best places cost absolutely nothing to visit. As you can see from the following pages, whatever your age and interests, whether you're a parent with children to entertain, a Londoner wanting to explore or a visitor to our great city, you really can do a lot of wonderful things here without paying a penny for the privilege.

Is everything in this book really absolutely free?

In a word, yes. Except where clearly stated to the contrary, everything in this book is completely free. The only qualification is that if an asterisk (*) appears next to a name, this means that free access is restricted in some way. The attraction may be free only at certain times (in which case, the times we give are only those when there is no charge), or, in a few cases, you may not have access to the whole building.

Just in case there is any confusion, where shops, markets, pubs or cafés are mentioned, they are included either because they offer great window-shopping opportunities or because we thought it would be helpful for you to know about them. Sadly, the goods and services they offer are not themselves free. Transport (Shanks's pony aside) also must be paid for. We would recommend any visitor to buy a London Transport Travelcard – they are very good value and, once you have bought one, you can zip around the capital with no regard to expense at all.

Organisation

How is the book laid out?

First, geographically – we've split London up into six areas. The first area is Central (which is mainly the area usually called the West End). The next three areas are West (starting at Hyde Park), North (starting at Regent's Park) and South (including everything south of the river). Going eastwards, we've subdivided the world into the City (EC postcodes) and the East End (E postcodes).

Secondly, as in England everything depends on the weather, we've divided each of the geographical sections into an outdoor section and an indoor section. The introduction to each chapter highlights the particular attractions of the area concerned and tells you where you can get more local information.

Each entry gives (as appropriate) an address, a telephone number and a map reference (eg 1–4D). We also give the nearest Tube station (or, if none, the nearest railway station) and the opening times.

We have given the most up-to-date information available, but details change and it's always a good idea to call ahead to check opening times and any other details of particular interest. If you are making a special trip, you should always check out the arrangements applying over holiday periods – opening hours may be modified, of course, but there may also be special events worth knowing about. With the aid of a Mercury *one2one* phone, you can call all but a handful of the telephone numbers listed absolutely free of charge on the PersonalCall tariff, between 7 pm and 7 am, and all day at weekends.

At the back of the book, there's a list of all the parks, of all the museums, and so on and an alphabetical index.

We're very pleased, courtesy of Mercury *one2one,* to be bringing you this guide to London's many free pleasures. If you have any comments or suggestions for inclusions in a future edition, please don't hesitate to write to us.

Richard Harden   **Peter Harden**

Londonwide information

Introduction

A huge amount of free information about London is there for the taking. It's very difficult to find yourself far from a public library, and you don't, of course, need to be a resident of the area concerned to go and browse through their newspapers, listings magazines and guide books.

The most central comprehensive libraries are Westminster, just by Leicester Square (35 St Martin's Street, WC2), Victoria (160 Buckingham Palace Road, SW1), Chelsea (Old Town Hall, SW3), Kensington (Hornton Street, W8) and St Pancras (by the railway station, NW1) – consult the telephone directory to find out where your local library is (it will be under the name of the relevant borough).

Libraries are also a great place to find posters and leaflets about what's going on in your area, and if you want inspiration for some free things to do close to home, your local branch is almost certainly the best place to start.

Locals shouldn't overlook the tourist information offices, which often have a lot of information about what's going on in an area which is of just as much interest to Londoners as it is to visitors. In each of the area chapters, we've listed these offices.

The following services provide information on a pan-London basis.

Sources of information

London Tourist Board SW1
Victoria Station   2–4B
The headquarters of the LTB at Victoria Station welcomes hundreds of thousands of visitors every year. As a general source of free (and other), up-to-date information about the metropolis, you won't do better. The LTB has some branches, which we've listed in the appropriate areas. Neither head office nor the branches offers a telephone enquiry service – they do, however, offer a series of premium-rate recorded services. For a list of these, call 0171-971 0026. / Times: 08.00-19.00; Tube: Victoria.

British Travel Centre W1
12 Regent St   2–2C
As its name suggests, this office near Piccadilly Circus is a good source of information about Britain generally, as well as just about London. / Times: Mon-Fri 09.00-18.30, Sat & Sun 10.00-16.00; Tube: Piccadilly Circus.

The mobile phone • For everyday • For everyone

London Transport Enquiries
Victoria Station, SW1   0171-222 1234   2–4B
This 24-hour telephone service is an invaluable source of help for any queries about buses or tubes run by London Transport. Their office on the concourse of Victoria Station is an excellent source of maps and brochures to enable you to use public transport efficiently.
/ *Times: office open 08.15 (Sun 08.45)-19.30; Tube: Victoria.*

Disabled access
There are three services which are very helpful for disabled people who are exploring London.

General queries relating in any way to travel can be addressed to Tripscope (The Courtyard, Evelyn Road, London W4 5JL; tel 0181-994 9294). Information about London Transport can be had from the Unit for Disabled Passengers (55 Broadway, London SW1H 0BD; tel 0171-918 3312) – their guide "Access to the Underground" is available without charge.

To check out the details of the access arrangements for any place of entertainment or tourist attraction in London you can call Artsline (54 Chalton Street, London NW1 1HS; tel 0171-388 2227). Artsline also publishes a range of access guides, including ones to tourist attractions (nominal charge).

Capital helpline
0171-388 7575
Capital Radio's all-year information line will try to answer your question – however practical, or however offbeat it might be. At various times of year, Capital also offers special helplines (numbers vary) such as revision lines (before GCSEs) and the Christmas line – a useful source of information over the period when London closes up and dies from Christmas Eve to Boxing Day. Listen in to FM 95.8 for details of these occasional services.

Kidsline
0171-222 8070
Kidsline is a source of lots of suggestions of what to do with kids during the school holidays – free and otherwise.

Sportsline
0171-222 8000
If you have any query relating in the broadest way to sports facilities in and around London, you can call Sportsline.
/ *Times: Mon-Fri 10.00-18.00.*

TNT Southern Cross
It may not be quite as comprehensive as "Time Out" (free only on consultation in public libraries), but "TNT Southern Cross"– the weekly magazine for expat aussies and kiwis – is obtainable without any charge and does have quite good theatre, cinema and other events listings. It's got some quite good articles of general budget interest too. Pick a copy up from the publication's spiritual home – outside Earl's Court tube – or from street-dispensers throughout central London.

Books

This book is a general guide, designed as an introduction to the many free delights which London has to offer. There are of course many special interests which you can pursue in London without cost, upon which there is much more information available than we are able to set out here. The following are some of the most handy books currently in print (you can also borrow them from a library) which will give you more information.

The best, comprehensive, general guide is probably "Fodor's London Companion" (Louise Nicholson, 1993). As a walking guide to London's principal architectural and historic attractions, "London Step by Step" (Christopher Turner, 1988) is both handy and reasonably detailed. "London Museums and Collections" (edited by Scimone and Levey, 1989) provides an intelligent overview, without going into so much detail as to put off the general reader. "The London Market Guide" (Andrew Kershman, 1994) tells you everything you might want to know about that colourful area of street life, and "Outdoor London" (Sarah Brown, 1991) gives a detailed overview of the green spaces in and around the metropolis.

Galleries

Especially for Old Masters – but also for almost any other form of art – London remains, despite the economic ravages of the last few years, one of the great centres of the international market in pictures and objets d'art. Much of the business is conducted through galleries to which the public has free access.

We can't lead you to the changing artistic attractions of the capital, as many of the most interesting commercial shows last for only a month or so. Help is at hand, however, in the form of an excellent monthly publication – "Galleries" – of which you can obtain a copy, gratis, from almost any commercial art gallery. Its handy format contains a wealth of information, helpfully organised into areas (with maps) and indexed in every way you could possibly want (including by artist and type of work). It also contains short but interesting articles on many of the forthcoming attractions.

You could easily spend a week just exploring London's commercial galleries. As a starting point, the greatest concentrations are found around Cork Street, Bruton Street and Old Bond Street W1, and St James's SW1. There are also clusters of galleries around the junction of Portobello Road and Westbourne Grove W11, in Walton Street SW3, and to the north and east of the City.

The great auction houses are a fascinating part of the art world – details are given in the Central section.

Attractions all round London

Bus Tours

If, as we assume in the introduction, you already have a Travelcard, you can explore all over London from the very best possible vantage point – the upper platform of a double-decker bus – at absolutely no cost whatsoever. This form of tour has the virtue that you can "hop on and hop off" to your heart's content – if you find there are so many things to do that you don't have time to finish the planned circuit, it hardly matters.

With one of London Transport's free bus guides, you can, of course, plan your own tour, but there are two routes which are particularly suitable for a general orientation.

The number 11 takes you on a great East-West tour of London, and includes many of the major sights. Starting in Chelsea's fashionable King's Road, it takes you through Victoria to Westminster Abbey. This would be quite a good place to break the journey and to cover part of it on foot: through Parliament Square, and down Whitehall to have a look at 10 Downing Street and the Cenotaph. Hop back on the bus, which will take you through Trafalgar Square (with Nelson's Column and the National Gallery), down the Strand and Fleet Street and ending at St Paul's Cathedral or, if you stay on till the end of the journey, at Liverpool Street, in the commercial heart of the City.

The number 15 shares the Trafalgar Square to St Paul's section with the number 11 (so you can change at any point between the two). At the eastern (City) end of the number 15's route, however, you see the Monument, Tower Bridge and the the Tower of London (and, on a Sunday morning, you might press on to Aldgate, for the Petticoat Lane market). At the western end of its route, you go through the heart of "shoppers' London", taking in Piccadilly Circus, Regent Street and Oxford Street. If you avoid these opportunities to spend, spend, spend, you will end up in Notting Hill, one of the nicest parts of inner London for a walk (especially on Saturday, when the Portobello Road market is in full swing).

Courts

If you've half a day to kill, you might find it interesting, and perhaps amusing, to spend it in court. There are three types of court which will be within easy reach of most parts of London – magistrates, crown and county courts.

All human life passes through London's magistrate's courts, where the highest and the lowest appear to explain why they have (or have not) committed minor criminal offences, from drunkenness to speeding. Sometimes it will be pretty humdrum stuff (if not without human interest), but if you hit lucky, you may hit a real trial, probably not lasting more than a day, where the question "did he do it?" is of more than academic interest, especially to the person in the dock.

In the Crown courts, the more serious crimes – all the way up to murder – are tried by a judge and jury. The disadvantage for the casual visitor is that most trials go on for at least several days, so inevitably you will see only a fraction of the proceedings. By far the most interesting theatre is to be found when a witness (especially the defendant) is being cross-examined by the opposing side's bewigged counsel. The Old Bailey (see The City) is London's senior Crown court.

County Courts resolve civil disputes (usually, claims for damages). Again, cross-examination is generally by far the most gripping part of a trial. The most important civil trials take place at the Royal Courts of Justice (see The City).

For the address of your local court, consult the telephone directory. Courts generally sit between 10.00 and 16.30. Children under 16 are not generally admitted into the public galleries.

Fire Stations
It may be possible to organise a visit to your local fire station. Write to London Fire Brigade, Public Relations, 8 Albert Embankment, London SE1 7SD.

Regular events

All-year-round events

The following ceremonial events happen all through the year.

Ceremony of the Keys
Tower of London, EC3   0171-709 0765
Every night at 21.30, in accordance with seven centuries of tradition, the Tower of London (home, of course, to the Crown Jewels) is secured for the night with a brief ceremony. Anyone can apply for a ticket to attend, but you should give at least two months' notice. There are quite strict rules as to how you should go about applying, and the best course is to phone the number given for instructions. / Tube: Tower Hill.

Changing the Guard (Buckingham Palace)
Buckingham Palace, SW1
The famous changing of the sentries at Buckingham Palace takes place at 11.30 every other day. The new guard, leaves Wellington Barracks three minutes before the change, and, preceded by a band, marches down Birdcage Walk to the palace. The ceremony itself lasts 40 minutes, and takes place inside the railings of the palace itself. The event is subject to cancellation in bad weather, or during state visits. / Tube: Green Park.

Changing the Guard (Horse Guards)
Horse Guards Parade, SW1
In a daily burst of pageantry, a mounted guard leaves Hyde Park Barracks at 10.28 (Sun 09.28) and proceeds, via Hyde Park Corner and Constitution Hill to arrive at Horse Guards Parade at 11.00 (Sun 10.00), where the guard is changed. The splendidly attired mounted guardsmen making their way through Hyde Park offers one of London's most romantic sights. / Tube: Hyde Park Corner, St James's Park.

Gun Salutes
One of the most striking sights in London is the gun salutes which hail royal and state events. These take place both in Hyde Park (12.00) and at the Tower of London (13.00) on the following dates (or, if a Sunday, the following day): 6 February (Accession Day); 21 April (the Queen's birthday); 2 June (Coronation Day); 10 June (the Duke of Edinburgh's birthday); and 4 August (the Queen Mother's birthday). Salutes also mark state visits (usually in May and October), Trooping the Colour (June) and the State Opening of Parliament (October or November). / Tube: Hyde Park Corner, Tower Hill.

The mobile phone • For everyday • For everyone

Annual diary

Barely a month goes by in London without some great event happening, which can provide a good focus for a day out, especially with children in tow. The major events which happen on an annual basis are as follows.

January

London Parade
The New Year starts with a bang, in the form of a big parade on the first day of the year. It starts from Parliament Square at noon, and the final band reaches Berkeley Square in Mayfair around 14.45. The procession (for which Whitehall or Piccadilly are the best vantage-points) consists of marching bands, floats and horse-drawn carriages, in which ride the mayors of Westminster and of all the London boroughs (but not, of course, the fiercely independent City).
/ Tube: Westminster, Embankment, Green Park.

Chinese New Year
In late January or early February, Chinatown celebrates the Chinese New Year with noisy, colourful parades (including the famous papier mâché dragons), which last most of the day. The whole area (around Gerrard Street, W1) is brightly decorated for the event.
/ Tube: Leicester Square.

March

Head of the River Race
0181-940 2219
The Oxford and Cambridge Boat Race may be more famous, but for the casual observer, the Head of the River race, which is rowed on a Saturday in March from Mortlake to Putney, may be more interesting to watch. The sheer number of crews (usually over 400) means that the colourful procession of eight-oared boats (which are set off 10 seconds apart) takes well over an hour. Being a timed race, it does have the disadvantage that no one knows who has won until it's all over. Best vantage points are as for the Boat Race (below). / Tube: Putney Bridge.

April

Kite Festival
Blackheath, SE3
Easter Sunday and Monday see London's leading annual kite festival – a great spectacle whether you're interested in kite-flying or not. (Devotees might like to note that there are also two smaller events in the summer – here and in Hackney Marshes). / Brit Rail: Blackheath.

London Marathon
0171-620 4117

The London Marathon, first run in 1981, has grown into a huge event which attracts more than 20,000 runners and over a million spectators annually. Its sheer scale and spectacle makes it a good family day out. The course of just over 26 miles begins (around 09.00) in Greenwich and ends (having taken a circuitous route) outside Buckingham Palace. The leading runners take a little over a couple of hours to complete the course, but the stragglers ensure that it's practically an all-day event.

Oxford and Cambridge Boat Race
It may be an arcane and thoroughly English way of spending an afternoon, but the world's most famous boat-race, first rowed on the Thames in 1849, continues to exercise an extraordinary grip on the popular imagination, and tens of thousands of people turn out every year to snatch a passing glimpse of an 18 minute race, which, from a practical point of view, is much better watched on television. The best vantage points from which to watch part of the 4 mile race from Putney to Mortlake are generally held to be at the half-way point (Hammersmith) or at the finish – but you don't get much of a view anywhere and the real point is not really the race but the atmosphere. Take a picnic – and, if you want to know who's won, a radio. / Tube: Putney Bridge.

May

Covent Garden Festival
Covent Garden, WC2   0171-240 0560

During the Covent Garden festival, a stage is put up at the west end of the Piazza, and a whole range of short choral and theatrical works is performed. Call the number given for the festival brochure.
/ Tube: Covent Garden.

June

City of London Festival
City Festival Box Office, St Paul's Churchyard, London EC4M 8BU   0171-377 0540

In late June/early July the City enjoys an explosion of music. If you're looking for free events, seek out the "Fringe" brochure – there's not much alternative about it, but it's where most of the no-charge events are listed. In it, you will find, on any one weekday, up to half a dozen lunchtime concerts in churches – all without charge, though contributions to the retiring collection will be welcome. The Festival's "Opening Service" (morning) is effectively a sung eucharist followed by a free choral concert in the magnificent setting of St Paul's. There is almost invariably a charge for the evening events.

Greenwich Festival
0181-305 1818

"Could this be London's Edinburgh?", muse the organisers of South London's great early-June arts festival – it's not quite there yet, but there's a whole range of attractions, many of which are free. There are, for example, the opening night celebrations with fireworks, and open-air jazz concerts. The Oxleas Festival, a celebration of the famous ancient woodland now saved from the builders, takes place at about the same time. / *Brit Rail:* Greenwich.

Trooping the Colour
0171-930 4466

A Saturday in early June sees the celebration of the Queen's Official Birthday, when she inspects an elaborate military display at Horse Guards Parade, SW1. At 13.00, after her return to Buckingham Palace, there is an RAF flypast down the Mall. There is a charge to attend the event itself (although, of course, you can watch the procession down the Mall), but tickets for the first rehearsal (two or three Saturdays before) are free, and (as for the main event itself) are allocated by ballot. Apply in good time, with a stamped addressed envelope, to Brigade Major (Trooping the Colour), Headquarters, Household Division, Horse Guards, Whitehall, London SW1A 2AX. / *Tube:* St James's Park.

Henley Royal Regatta
01491-572153

Henley, established in 1839, is the world's oldest major rowing regatta. Even if you've never been in a rowing boat in your life, and even if you don't know anyone who is a member of one of the enclosures, it's still one of the most enjoyable events of the "Season" and manages, to an extraordinary extent, to maintain something of the atmosphere of an Edwardian carnival. Take a picnic, arrive early, and find a good viewpoint along the towpath – all but the last third of a mile or so of the course is open to the public, and at many points you can hear the commentary. The event lasts from a Wednesday to Sunday in late June/early July – it's much less crowded on the weekdays. / *Brit Rail:* Henley.

Swan Upping
0171-236 1863
All the swans on the Thames between London Bridge and Henley belong to the Queen, and one of two of the City Livery Companies: the Dyers' or the Vintners'. This cosy three-way arrangement has been in place since 1510.

Each year, it is necessary to mark the cygnets to show to whom they belong (which depends, of course, on who owns their parents). This task is carried out every July, by a procession of six "Thames Skiffs" (rowed by colourfully uniformed oarsmen), which takes a week to progress from Sunbury to Sonning. When swans are spotted, the traditional cry of "All-up" is raised, and they are corralled by three skiffs, one manned by each of the potential owners, in preparation for identification and marking (or not, as appropriate – Her Majesty's swans, like her motor cars, are unmarked). The swans, it seems, do not always come quietly. If you want to know when and where you can witness this extraordinary annual ritual, call the Vintners on the number given.

Notting Hill Carnival
The August Bank holiday sees the largest street-party in Europe – a million people attending a noisy celebration of Afro-Caribbean culture. The events, centred around the northern parts of the Portobello Road, take place over the Sunday and the Monday, with the second day seeing the carnival procession proper. It's certainly impressive in its sheer scale and vitality, but this may make it seem rather daunting to some people. All the common-sense rules of attending such a large and crowded occasion apply – don't drive to it, keep hold of children, and carry as little money as possible. All of the festivities happen during the day, and it's best not to hang around in the evening. / Tube: Notting Hill Gate, Ladbroke Grove.

Covent Garden Festival of Street Theatre
Covent Garden, WC2
For two weeks in September, Covent Garden Market celebrates street theatre, with a range of high quality acts throughout the day. / Tube: Covent Garden.

Great River Race
c/o Stuart Wolff 0181-398 9057

Still a relative newcomer (it began in 1988), this ever more popular event has all the ingredients of a Great British Success Story. For a start, the idea behind it is completely – inspiringly – batty. Take over 200 oared boats (rule: no racing-boats allowed), devise a handicapping system (which allows some boats to start 100 minutes before others) and set them off on a 22 mile journey from Ham House in Richmond to Island Gardens, on the Isle of Dogs. The event attracts every type of boat (from Chinese dragon boats to Hawaiian war canoes) and rowers of every age and degree of seriousness from all over the world. It's a wonderful spectacle, and one which can be viewed from any London bank of the Thames (though the greatest excitement is of course at the start and the finish). / Tube: Putney Bridge.

National Trust Free Entry Day

There's generally a charge to enter National Trust properties, but on one day a year (and in 1995 it will be 13 September), many properties are open free of charge. Needless to say, if you value tranquillity, this is probably not the best time to go, but the day does offer an opportunity to explore the delights of properties such as Osterley Park House in Middlesex, Sutton House in Surrey and Ham House in Richmond. Confirm a property's participation in the scheme before setting off.

Raising of the Thames Barrier
Unity Way, SE18   0181-854 1373

Canute was wrong – you can hold back the tide, but only by spending half a billion pounds on a great river barrier, designed to protect central London from the ever-growing risk of flooding. The Thames Barrier (see also) is a miracle of modern engineering (completed in 1982). Once a year (usually in September or October) there is a full test and all ten of the massive steel gates are raised against the high tide. Call the Visitor Centre for details. / Brit Rail: Charlton.

London Thames Festival

A proposed newcomer for 1995 (and expected to be a bi-annual event) in celebration of the 22 miles of the River Thames which run through the capital. "London's natural park", as it is sometimes called, does not receive the attention it deserves, and this wide-ranging event (based around the South Bank Centre) is intended to help remedy this deficiency.

October

Punch and Judy Festival
Covent Garden, WC2

The first Sunday of October sees a plethora of Punch and Judy shows, and their continental equivalents – Polichinelle (France), Kasper (Germany) and Pulcinella (Italy). / Tube: Covent Garden.

State Opening of Parliament

If you want to see the Queen, wearing a crown, and riding in a gilded coach, the only annual opportunity to do so is the State Opening of Parliament (usually in October). Her Majesty rides from Buckingham Palace to Westminster to deliver the Queen's Speech (which sets out the government's legislative plans for the forthcoming year, and is, in fact, written by the Prime Minister) and then returns to her palace. As an event, it's not hugely well attended, and offers possibly the best "royal-watching" opportunity of the year. / Tube: Westminster.

November

Fireworks Night

The annual remembrance of the failure of the Gunpowder plot (when Guy Fawkes and his merry men attempted, in 1605, to blow up monarch, lords and commons assembled at Westminster) is celebrated with a huge number of bonfire and firework parties of all sizes all over London. Parties take place on November 5 itself and, if it falls mid-week, the weekends before and after. The larger events are widely advertised on posters and in local newspapers – Battersea Park and Primrose Hill are two of the biggest regular parties.

Lord Mayor's Show

The Lord Mayor's Show has taken place – plague permitting – in some form in most years since 1215. It celebrates the annual presentation of the new Lord Mayor of London to the Queen's Justices. This formerly took place at Westminster, but now involves a rather shorter journey to the Royal Courts of Justice in the Strand.

The show takes place on the second Saturday of November. It begins at the Guildhall at 11.00 and its heart is a 1 1/2 mile long procession, which includes 60 floats, 20 bands and about 5,000 people. The centrepiece of the procession is the Lord Mayor's gilded, eighteenth century coach, pulled by six shire horses.

This is a great traditional Londoners' day out – a whole day's entertainment is provided, ending with a firework display over the Thames - and about a quarter of a million people attend annually. Many City attractions which are generally closed at the weekends open on the day of the show. / Tube: Bank.

RAC London to Brighton Veteran Car Run

Saturday 14 November 1896 was a great day in the history of British motoring – for the first time it was legal to proceed at more than 4 mph and without being preceded by a man with a red flag. Ever since (war years excepted) horseless carriages have taken part in an annual celebration of automobile "Emancipation". The Run – it is NOT a race – takes place on the first Sunday in November, leaving Hyde Park at 07.30, and progressing via Westminster (07.35) and Lambeth Town Hall (07.45) to Brighton, where the front-runners arrive around 10.30. Only cars built before 1905 are eligible to take part, and competitors come from all over the world. Over a million people watch the Run each year – 1996, being the centenary, will no doubt attract a bumper crowd. / Tube: Hyde Park Corner.

Remembrance Sunday
Whitehall, SW1
The Sunday nearest 11 November sees the most sober, and the most moving, large-scale event of the year. Just after 11.00, the Queen and representatives of the government and the Commonwealth lay wreaths of Flanders poppies on the Cenotaph to commemorate those who gave their lives in war. After the short service, the tone becomes a little lighter as the veterans march past.
/ Tube: *Embankment, Charing Cross, Westminster.*

Christmas Parade
A major new event in 1994, this American-style parade (with marching bands and floats) around the main shopping streets of the West End will happen on a Sunday late every November. If it even begins to live up to the aspirations which the organisers have for it, it will fast become one of the big events of the year. / Tube: *Oxford Circus, Piccadilly Circus, Bond Street.*

December

Christmas Lights
The heartland of London's shopping – Oxford Street, Regent Street and, in a rather more subdued way, Bond Street – generally puts on a reasonable show with its Christmas lights. The illuminations are given a celebrity "switch on" in November, and they are there to be admired until Twelfth Night. An evening visit to this part of town around this time also permits some vigorous window-shopping at Selfridges and the other stores of Oxford Street, and Hamleys and Liberty on Regent Street. Simpson and Fortnum & Mason on Piccadilly usually put on a pretty good display as well. Do note that, in the run-up to Christmas, the whole of the centre of the West End can be surprisingly crowded well after the shops have closed.
/ Tube: *Oxford Circus, Bond Street.*

Christmas Tree
Trafalgar Square, WC2
The great Christmas Tree in Trafalgar Square, decorated with its bright white lamps, is an annual gift from the people of Oslo to the people of London. There are regular carol concerts around the tree.
/ Tube: *Charing Cross.*

New Year's Eve
Trafalgar Square, WC2
Packing yourself into Trafalgar Square is traditionally the way to see in the New Year in London. Those who do not like crowds should definitely stay away, and even those who do should think twice – as midnight approaches the drunken crush can be absolutely unbearable and it can be so crowded as to be impossible to get into the Square itself. Getting home is, unusually, free of charge as London Transport operate their annual (usually sponsored) offer of free transport throughout the capital, with the tube running well past midnight. / Tube: *Charing Cross.*

Entertainments

Radio & TV
audience participation

London's position as a great centre of broadcasting means
that there's a huge amount of entertainment of almost every
kind — from classical concerts to gameshows — just there
for the asking, since being a member of the studio audience
at such events is almost invariably free.

In this chapter, we have given the details of the people who
organise recitals, concerts and TV and radio programmes.
It's worth remembering that, even for radio and TV, it's
surprising what you may be able to pick up at short notice.

Radio – BBC

Radio Ticket Unit, BBC, London W1A 4WW   Recorded
information 0171-765 5858; enquiries 0171-765 5243
*Radio shows tend to be scheduled only about 6 weeks ahead. The
recorded information service tells you what's on offer (it's on
CEEFAX too) or you can get information by post. For a one-off query
send an sae, but they will, on request, put your name on a mailing
list and you will be kept up to date with what's available. There's
something for almost all tastes, from classical concerts (BBCSO), via
easy listening to quiz programmes. Shows are mainly recorded at the
following venues: the Paris Studio, Regent Street SW1; the Concert
Hall at Broadcasting House W1; the Hippodrome, North End Road
NW11; and the Maida Vale Studios, Delaware Road W9.*

Radio – Capital

Euston Tower, London NW1 3DR   0171-608 6080
*If you want to get close to the stars — especially of the teenybopper
variety — Capital Radio's open air roadshows are for you. There are
four of them around London in the earlier part of the summer. They
last all afternoon, with one of the hit groups of the moment at the
top of the bill. Listen in for details and take a picnic for a fun day
out.*

Television – BBC

Ticket Unit, Room 301, Design Building, Television Centre
London W12 7RJ   0181-576 1227
*There's a huge choice of comedies, variety shows, quiz programmes
and debates which you can go and watch being recorded. Send an
sae to the Ticket Unit, and they will send you clearly organised sheets
about what's on offer — it's helpful to them if you can give a general
indication of the sort of programme you're interested in. People
sometimes drop out at short notice, and it may be worth trying even
for shows happening in the near future. Parties are welcome and this
is an ideal outing for all ages that costs no more than the coach hire.
Children aged less than 14 are not generally admitted.*

Television – ITV

Many of the most popular independent TV shows, are filmed at the London TV Centre on the South Bank. The Ticket Office (tel 0171-261 3971/3447) deals with some (but not all) of the shows recorded there, and with some which are recorded elsewhere.

Many ITV (and also now some BBC) programmes are made by relatively small, independent production companies and some of them have a policy of advertising for audience participants when (and only when) they want to recruit them. For these, it's worth keeping an eye on the media – Time Out and Private Eye are apparently favoured – especially in the Autumn.

There is a firm which specialises in finding audiences, and maintains a mailing list. It is Inspired PR of 9 Crondal Place, Edgbaston, Birmingham B15 2LB (tel 0121-440 1633). They are employed by some of the smaller, independent TV production companies, and are often looking for people in the London area, frequently for programmes recorded at the old Thames Studios at Teddington. Send them an sae for details of forthcoming shows.

If you really want to see a particular programme, there's no substitute for tracking down the production company concerned and asking them how they allocate their tickets.

Music

City music

There is music in one of the many churches of the City almost every lunchtime – almost all concerts begin between 13.00 and 13.15 and generally last no more than an hour. A useful monthly publication, "City Events", available from the City of London Information Centre by St Paul's gives advance details. Alternatively, if you arrive at the Information Office by 12.40, you should have time to locate the concert of your choice and walk to the appropriate church.

The top time of year for City music is during the City of London Festival (see also) in late June/early July.

The Corporation of London also presents a series of band concerts through the summer at four locations (Finsbury Circus, Tower Place, Royal Exchange Forecourt and St Paul's Cathedral Steps) from 12.00 to 14.00 on Wednesdays and Thursdays from June to September – you can get a leaflet from the Information Centre. During the summer, Broadgate (see also) is another regular music spot.

Events in the Royal Parks
Most of the Royal Parks (Hyde, St James's, Green, Greenwich and Richmond Parks, and Kensington Gardens) have music on a regular basis and it's well worth sending an A5 stamped addressed envelope to Old Police House, Hyde Park, London W2 2UH (tel 0171-298 2000), asking for one of the "Summer Entertainment Programmes". Events of interest to adults extend well beyond music, and include theatrical and operatic productions, dancing demonstrations and guided nature and gardening tours of the parks. For children, there are circus acts and puppet shows.

Music colleges
London boasts some of the finest music colleges in the world and, to those who enjoy classical music they represent an extremely fertile source of free entertainment.

All the schools listed below give three or four concerts or recitals a week during their term-time. The most popular performances tend to be the larger ones – those with symphony orchestras or works with a large chorus – of which there may be five or so in a term at a given school.

Guildhall School of Music and Drama * EC2
Silk Street, Barbican   0171-628 2571   5–1C
Events take place at the school, at the Barbican and elsewhere. A termly programme gives full details. / Tube: Moorgate.

Royal Academy of Music, NW1
Marylebone Road   0171-873 7373   2–1A
Most performances are given around 13.00 in the college's Dukes Hall. / Tube: Baker Street.

Royal College of Music SW7
Kensington Church Street   0171-589 3643, x 4380   3–1B
The college is located just behind the Royal Albert Hall. Most of the performances are given at the college, though quite a number are given at other venues around the capital – at 13.10 on Fridays, during term, a concert is given at the imposing church of St Mary Abbots in the centre of Kensington. / Tube: South Kensington.

Trinity College of Music W1
11 Mandeville Place   0171-935 5773   2–1A
Most concerts and recitals, here, take place around 13.00, either in their Barbirolli Lecture Hall or the nearby Hinde Street church. / Tube: Bond Street.

Other Venues
Most of the major arts centres offer free foyer music (often of very high quality) on a regular basis – details are given under the entries for the respective venues. See the Royal Festival Hall (South), the Royal National Theatre (South), and the Barbican (City). Other places listed which offer regular free music are Westminster Abbey (Central), St Mary Abbots (West) and Union Chapel (North).

Shell LSO Music Scholarship Final
Barbican Concert Hall   0171-638 8891
The £6,000 Shell LSO Music Scholarship is one of the most prestigious prizes available to young musicians. The competition final is held in late June/early July each year and involves the LSO performing selected movements with the four competitors, who are in their late teens/early 20s. It's a very enjoyable event if you prefer listening to classical music in a very informal atmosphere. Tickets are allocated on a first-come, first-served basis by the Barbican Box Office – contact the number given, or for more information call the LSO Scholarship Administrator on 0171-588 1116.
/ Tube: Barbican, Moorgate.

Opera

Covent Garden – Big Screen on the Piazza WC2
Covent Garden   2–2C
Two or three nights a year – the events are widely advertised at the time – the Royal Opera relays the performance taking place inside the Opera House on a big screen outside. You have to stand, of course, but it's a great way of spending an evening. If there's a big star appearing, you had better arrive early if you want a good position.

Central London

Introduction

The fact that Central London is at the ceremonial and governmental heart of Britain – including as it does the Houses of Parliament, Westminster Abbey, Buckingham Palace and 10 Downing Street – provides an almost unequalled range of famous historic attractions. The Abbey and, with planning, Parliament can both be visited.

Art and antiquities is another major theme of the area, which contains some of the most significant museums and art galleries in the world. In the mega-league are the British Museum, the National Gallery and the Tate Gallery. There are, however, also some smaller attractions which still have absolutely first-rate collections – among these, the Wallace Collection and Sir John Soane's Museum stand out. In addition, the commercial art world provides a huge and ever-changing selection of pictures and objects to view, and the institutions which deal in them have their own special interest and charm. A visit to one of the great auctioneers, such as Sotheby's and Christie's combines art with theatre. For a guide to the commercial galleries (see "Galleries" on page 16).

The area is a window-shopper's paradise, containing as it does most of the UK's top shops – ranging from Harrods, Selfridges and Fortnum & Mason at the larger end of the scale to the opulent boutiques of Bond Street, and the charming, small shops in the Regency Burlington Arcade. Almost all of the very central areas have sufficient character to justify just strolling around, but Covent Garden would probably be on most lists.

With children, this is a rather tiring area. There are the sights of course – one can add Trafalgar Square and Eros to those already mentioned – and there is also the ultimately demanding possibility of a trip to Hamleys, the toy shop. Leaving this aside, the top attractions for families are probably St James's Park – which is pretty and interesting enough to provide something for everyone – and Coram's Fields, a great amenity for kids, in Bloomsbury.

London Tourist Board SW1
Victoria Station   2–4B
The headquarters of the tourist board are in front of Victoria Station. / Times: 08.00-19.00; Tube: Victoria.

Selfridges W1
400 Oxford Street   2–2A
The Oxford Street branch of the London Tourist Board is in the basement of the department store. / Times: Mon-Sat 09.30-19.00 (Thu 20.00); Tube: Bond Street.

The mobile phone • For everyday • For everyone

Indoor attractions

Alfred Dunhill SW1

30 Duke Street   0171-499 9566   2–3B

Jermyn Street, London's most discreet shopping thoroughfare, boasts the headquarters of one of the great success stories of international luxury branded goods. In their opulent premises, the All Nations Pipe Collection is displayed, including curiosities such as a rare carved slate pipe from Queen Charlotte Islands and a carved meerschaum pipe with a bowl 18 inches in length, depicting a nineteenth century royal wedding. If you give at least 48 hours notice (ask for the Archive) you can visit the Alfred Dunhill Museum, intriguingly located at 60/61 Burlington Arcade W1, which houses examples of motoring accessories, lighters, watches, pens and leathergoods manufactured by Dunhill over the last century. / Times: *Mon-Sat 09.30 (Sat 10.00)-18.00;* Tube: *Green Park, Piccadilly Circus.*

Architectural Association WC1

34-36 Bedford Square   0171-636 0974   2–1C

For anyone with an interest in architecture, the Association offers a rich and varied programme of afternoon and evening lectures, as well as a gallery which holds a number of exhibitions annually. / Times: *Mon-Fri 10.00-19.00, Sat 10.00-15.00;* Tube: *Tottenham Court Road.*

Architecture Foundation SW1

The Economist Building, 30 Bury Street   0171-839 9389   2–3B

This relatively recently established body is "dedicated to the display and discussion of contemporary architecture and the built environment". In addition to their exhibition programme, they hold a series of forums on architectural and urban planning questions, to which the public are invited. / Times: *Tue, Wed & Fri 12.00-18.00; Thu 14.00-18.00; Sat & Sun 14.00-18.00;* Tube: *Green Park.*

Ben Uri Art Society W1

4th Floor, 21 Dean Street   0171-437 2852   2–2C

Displays from the Society's permanent collection of over 800 works by Jewish artists (including Bomberg, Auerbach, Epstein and Kitaj) are complemented by changing, temporary exhibitions of contemporary art at this Soho gallery. / Times: *Mon-Thu 10.00-17.00 Sun (during exhibitions) 14.00-17.00; closed Jewish holidays;* Tube: *Tottenham Court Road, Leicester Square.*

British Dental Association Museum W1

64 Wimpole Street   0171-935 0875 x 209   2–1B

If you have an interest in the macabre, why not explore the history of British dentistry since the eighteenth century. The association's extensive museum features equipment, furniture, re-created surgeries and cartoon prints. / Times: *Mon-Fri 09.30-16.00;* Tube: *Oxford Circus, Regent's Park, Bond Street.*

The mobile phone · For everyday · For everyone

British Museum WC1
Great Russell Street   0171-636 1555   2–1C

Six million visitors a year can't be wrong – this august neo-classical building (Robert Smirke, 1823-52) is London's leading attraction – free or otherwise. It does, after all, house what is arguably the world's greatest collection of antiquities. Particular strengths include Egyptian antiquities, coins and medals, the collections relating to Greek and Roman civilisation (especially, of course, the marbles from the Parthenon), clocks, and prints and drawings. No one could possibly take in the whole museum in a day – just to pass by all the exhibits would apparently require a walk of some 2 1/2 miles – so it's probably worth deciding on a section of particular interest and trying to make sense of that. From Tue-Sat, the museum's experts give gallery talks at 11.30, and lectures at 13.15. There are many interesting temporary exhibitions (mostly free of charge) and there are regular talks and films, and even occasional art workshops for children. / Times: Mon-Sat 10.00-17.00, Sun 14.30-18.00; Tube: Russell Square, Tottenham Court Road, Holborn.

Burlington Arcade W1
Between Piccadilly and Burlington Gardens   2–2B

This Regency shopping arcade is perhaps the most timeless place in London for window-shopping. Top-hatted beadles maintain standards – no running, no singing, no carrying large parcels etc – leaving you in perfect serenity to survey the displays in the windows of the small, elegant shops, many of which still sell hand-made luxury goods. / Times: Mon-Sat 09.00-17.30; Tube: Green Park, Piccadilly Circus.

Christie's SW1
8 King Street   0171-839 9060   2–3B

The two great international auction-houses (the other, of course, is Sotheby's, which has its own entry below) are both based in London. Christie's has been helping the aristocracy build up, and, in later generations dispose of, great collections of pictures and furniture since 1766. Except for their very, very grandest sales (for which admission is restricted to those who have bought catalogues), you are welcome to have a look at the goods to be auctioned in the four days before the sale and, indeed, to attend the auction itself – one of the best free shows in town. / Times: Mon- Fri 9.30-16.30 (Tue 20.00), Sun 14.00-16.30; Tube: Green Park.

Flaxman Gallery WC1
University Coll, Gower St   0171-387 7050 x 7793   2–1C

John Flaxman (1755-1826) was a pre-eminent name in the emergence of neo-classicism in England and was, in 1810, appointed the first Professor of Sculpture at the Royal Academy. The gallery, which displays many of the plaster models from which the marble sculptures were eventually made, was inaugurated in 1857. / Times: Mon-Thu 8.45-10.30, Fri 8.45-19.00, Sat 09.30-16.30; Tube: Warren Street, Goodge Street.

The mobile phone • For everyday • For everyone

Fortnum & Mason W1

181 Piccadilly   0171-734 8040   2–2B

The royal grocers (established on this site in 1707) have all the accoutrements you could possibly desire of such an establishment – plush red carpets, glittering chandeliers and assistants in tailcoats. The shop has particularly impressive displays of its famous produce, both in the splendid ground floor sales area and in the Piccadilly windows. The shop's clock is famous – see the outdoor section.
/ *Times:* Mon-Sat 09.30-18.00; *Tube:* Green Park, Piccadilly Circus.

Foyle's WC2

113-119 Charing Cross Road   0171-437 5660   2–2C

You can potter happily for hours in Britain's biggest bookshop – an establishment which carries a copy of almost every book in print, however esoteric (though actually finding any given title can prove a little difficult). / *Times:* Mon-Sat 09.00-18.00 (19.00 Thu); *Tube:* Tottenham Court Road.

Freemasons' Hall WC2

Great Queen Street   0171-831 9811   2–2D

If you have always been fascinated by the aura of secrecy of Freemasonry, it may come as a surprise that the Masons are very pleased for you to visit their daunting Grand Temple in Covent Garden. The current monolith was dedicated in 1933, but the site has been associated with Freemasonry for over two centuries. The Library and Museum (with collections of plate, glassware, jewels and regalia) are open to the public, and there are hourly tours (from 11.00 to 16.00, not 13.00) of the magnificent Temple.
/ *Times:* Mon-Fri 10.00-17.00; Sat 10.00-13.00; Closed Bank Hols and preceding Sats; *Tube:* Holborn, Covent Garden.

Hamleys W1

188 Regent Street   0171-734 3161   2–2B

Around Christmas it's unbearably crowded, but all year round this is the number one destination on any child's tour of London – the world's largest toyshop. / *Times:* Mon-Sat 10.00-19.00 (sometimes longer hours), Sun 12.00-18.00; *Tube:* Piccadilly Circus, Oxford Circus.

Harrods SW1

Knightsbridge   0171-730 1234   3–1D

Europe's most famous department store works very hard to ensure that there is always something new to see in its 25 acres of sales space. First-time visitors should not miss the Food Halls, with their intriguing décor and amazing arrangements of produce, but it is the sheer scale of the whole building and the opulence of some of the goods which are probably the main attractions. Special exhibitions are sometimes organised in the ground floor Central Hall. Harrods is becoming a little sensitive about its role as a free tourist attraction – parties of four or more are not admitted, dress should be appropriate and photography is not allowed. / *Times:* Mon, Tue & Sat 10.00-18.00, Wed-Fri 10.00-19.00; *Tube:* Knightsbridge.

Harvey Nichols SW1
Knightsbridge   0171-235 5000   3–1D
Harvey Nichols is a smaller, more intimate department store than its better known Knightsbridge neighbour and not, therefore, quite as suited to sight-seeing. Their particularly innovative window-displays are always interesting, though, and the glamorous new foodie complex on the fifth floor is worth a look for the sheer improbability of its "Dan Dare" style architecture and location.
/ *Times:* Mon-Fri 10.00-19.00 (Wed 20.00), Sat 10.00-18.00; *Tube:* Knightsbridge.

Houses of Parliament SW1
0171-219 4272   2–3C
No visitor will wish to miss the sight of the Palace of Westminster, with its famous clock tower (whose bell is known as Big Ben). There has been a royal palace here since the eleventh century, but, after a disastrous fire in 1835, the building was reconstructed in neo-Gothic style to the designs of Charles Barry and Augustus Pugin. Only Westminster Hall (facing Parliament Green) retains a significant medieval element.

The building is not generally open to the public, but if you want to see the fine interior – or our ancient democracy at work – there are two ways of going about it. One is to arrange to go on a tour, and the other is to watch a debate – in the Commons or Lords (from one of the Strangers' Galleries) or in a Commons committee. Dealing with the former first, UK citizens wanting to have a tour must apply to their MP in writing, and should do so well in advance. Citizens of other countries may apply, in writing, to the Public Information Office of the House of Commons (and may be accommodated at shorter notice).

If you want to watch a debate in progress, the galleries are open to the public. However, priority is given to those with tickets, and the safest course, therefore, to avoid a lengthy queue, is to apply for a ticket, as far in advance as possible, to your MP (or, if you are not a UK citizen, to your embassy or High Commission). Impromptu visitors have a good chance of gaining admission (unless the subject of debate is very controversial) later on in the day – sittings usually go on until 22.00, and sometimes beyond – or on Friday.
If you're planning any visit to Parliament, it's a very good idea to check out your plans with the Public Information Office on the number given. / *Tube:* Westminster.

Liberty W1
210-220 Regent's Street   0171-734 1234   2–2B
Liberty is one of the most charming and individualistic of London's department stores. It occupies very characterful mock-Tudor premises (built in the '20s, from timbers from men o'war), which are certainly worth a look. The store's particular strength is house furnishings and it carries many interesting and unusual objects and fabrics. / *Times:* Mon-Sat 09.30 (Wed 10.00)- 18.00 (Thu 19.30); *Tube:* Piccadilly Circus.

Museum of Mankind W1
6 Burlington Gardens   0171-437 2224   2–2B
*The Mayfair outpost of the British Museum is a huge Victorian
edifice (originally the HQ of London University), housing its collections
relating to non-Western societies and cultures. The changing
exhibitions are illustrated by occasional gallery talks and lectures.
Videos are shown Tue-Fri at 13.30 and 15.00.*
/ *Times:* Mon-Sat 10.00-17.00, Sun 14.30-18.00; Tube: *Piccadilly Circus.*

National Gallery WC2
Trafalgar Square   0171-389 1785
(recorded information 0171-839 3526)   2–2C
*One of the world's great galleries of Western European paintings,
from the late thirteenth century to the early twentieth – from Giotto
to Picasso. What distinguishes it is the balance of its collection across
all of the schools, with practically no great master unrepresented.
The once-controversial Sainsbury Wing (1991) houses the earliest
works (including Botticelli, Bellini, Raphael), and the rest of the
collection progresses chronologically through the West Wing
(Michelangelo, Holbein, Titian), the North Wing (Rubens, Velázquez,
Rembrandt) and the East Wing (Gainsborough, Turner, Constable,
Monet, van Gogh). The Beggruen collection, on long-term loan, beefs
up the gallery's own Post-Impressionists, and includes works by
Cézanne, Seurat and Braque. Tours of the collection take place two
or three times daily (Mon-Sat), according to the season, and there
are lectures at 13.00 (Tue-Fri) and 12.00 (Sat). At 13.00 on
Monday, there are films about artists or schools of painting. For
information, pick up a copy of The National Gallery News, and if you
prefer to let your fingers do the walking (or have a child of any age
to amuse), don't miss the Micro Gallery Computer Information
Room. There is a charge for some of the special exhibitions. Note
that the cloakrooms here will not keep packages or bags.*
/ *Times:* Mon-Sat 10.00-18.00, Sun 14.00-18.00; Tube: *Charing Cross,
Leicester Square.*

National Portrait Gallery WC2
2 St Martin's Place   0171-306 0055   2–2C
*This is arguably the most accessible of London's major galleries.
Though in most collections it's artistic merit which wins a place, here
it's the importance of the subject of the portrait as much as the
eminence of the painter, sculptor or photographer (though many of
the great British artists are, of course, represented). Almost all of the
major figures in English history are recorded, organised by period,
with the contemporary portraiture galleries being the most popular.
At 13.10 (Sat & Sun, 15.00) almost every day, there is a lecture
on some aspect of the collection. There is a variety of temporary
exhibitions, for some of which there is a charge.*
/ *Times:* Mon-Sat 10.00-18.00; Sun 12.00-18.00; Tube: *Leicester Square,
Charing Cross.*

The mobile phone • For everyday • For everyone

Percival David Foundation of Chinese Art WC1
53 Gordon Square   0171-387 3909   2–1C
The finest collection of Chinese ceramics outside China is not nearly
as well known as it deserves. There are approximately 1700 ceramic
items, reflecting Chinese court taste from the tenth to eighteenth
centuries. Two particular treasures are a unique pair of blue and
white temple vases, whose inscriptions date them to 1351.
/ Times: Mon-Fri 10.30-17.00; Tube: Russell Square, Goodge Street, Euston Square.

Petrie Museum of Egyptian Archaeology WC1
University College, Gower St   0171-387 7050 x 2884   2–1C
An extraordinary collection of Egyptian antiquities, excavated by the
eminent archaeologist Sir Flinders Petrie and his followers since
1884. The exhibition is organised to illustrate the development of
Egyptian culture from Palaeolithic to Roman times.
/ Times: Mon-Fri 10.00-12.00, 13.15-17.00; closed four weeks in
summer; occasionally open Sat; Tube: Warren Street, Goodge Street.

Phillips W1
101 New Bond Street   0171-629 6602   2–2B
It may be a little less well known than Sotheby's and Christie's, but
this Mayfair auctioneers offers just the same possibilities of getting
close to great (and lesser) works of art. (For an introduction to the
auction houses, see Christie's.) / Times: Mon-Fri 08.30-17.00;
Sun 14.00-17.00; Tube: Bond Street.

The Photographers' Gallery WC2
5 & 8 Great Newport Street   0171-831 1772   2–2C
This large, central gallery maintains an ever-changing programme of
photographic exhibitions. / Times: Mon-Sat 11.00-18.00;
Tube: Leicester Square.

Public Record Office WC2
Chancery Lane   0181-876 3444   2–2D
Treasures from among the national collection of documents are
displayed in the small museum of this fine neo-Gothic building near
the Law Courts. The highlight is the Domesday Book – the first
national census, carried out on the orders of William the Conqueror
in 1086 – with other records including Guy Fawkes's confession
(showing his signature before and after the thumb-screws were
applied) and Shakespeare's Will. (In late 1995 or early 1996, the
museum will close, pending relocation to the main office in Kew,
where a new museum is scheduled to open in 1997.)
/ Times: Mon-Fri 09.45-16.45; Tube: Chancery Lane.

RIBA Heinz Gallery W1
21 Portman Square   0171-580 5533   2–2A
This "darkly elegant" (to use their own phrase) room is the setting
for some interesting exhibitions, mainly of drawings from the British
Architectural Library's collection. The shows they organise – about
half a dozen a year – are diverse in their inspiration, and unlikely to
be so large as to overwhelm those without a specialist interest.
/ Times: Mon-Fri 11.00-17.00, Sat 10.00-13.00; Tube: Marble Arch, Baker Street.

Royal Academy of Arts * W1
Burlington House, Piccadilly   0171-439 7438   2–2B
Although there is a charge for all of the exhibitions (of which the most famous is the annual Summer Exhibition), there is no charge for access to the Academy's charming building, and two of its greatest attractions – one architectural, one artistic – which are always on view, gratis. The recent Sackler Galleries are reckoned by many to be one of the most successful modern additions to any period London building. The glass-sided lift, by which the new galleries are approached, offers a magical journey from the old to the new, and some of the Academy's sculptures are dramatically displayed outside the galleries. At the far end, in its own white space, is displayed the Academy's greatest artistic treasure, the Michelangelo Tondo – the only example in England of the master's sculpture. There are periodic free tours of the early eighteenth century Private Rooms, which are in some ways the most characterful part of the Academy – phone for details. / Times: 10.00-18.00; Tube: Piccadilly Circus, Green Park.

Royal Courts of Justice WC2
Strand   0171-936 6000   2–2D
Almost all of the most important civil cases in England and Wales end up being tried in this imposing Victorian Gothic building. There are usually at least 50 courts sitting at any one time, so you should be able to find something of interest – trials might cover anything from allocating fault for a serious accident to esoteric "administrative" law cases, in which people can challenge the government's exercise of its powers. Children under 16 are not admitted. / Times: Mon-Fri 10.00-16.30; Tube: Temple.

Royal Institute of British Architects W1
66 Portland Place   0171-580 5533   2–1B
There are three galleries at the Architecture Centre, which accommodates a wide range of architectural exhibitions. (See also Heinz Gallery.) / Times: Mon-Fri 10.00-17.30 (21.00 on lecture nights), Sat 10.00-13.00; Tube: Oxford Circus, Great Portland Street, Regent's Park.

Royal Institution * W1
21 Albemarle St   0171-409 2992   2–2B
As they are often televised, you may well have seen the annual Christmas lectures which are given at this huge Mayfair institution (where Faraday 'discovered' electricity). While there is a charge for these lectures, the society provides a couple of free lunchtime talks every year on scientific subjects of general interest (recent subjects have included creation and the Big Bang; genetics; and the weather). They run from 13.00-13.40 and there is usually one in November and one in March. / Tube: Green Park.

Royal Society of Art WC2

8 John Adam St   0171-930 5115   2–2C

The Royal Society for the encouragement of Arts, Manufactures and Commerce (to give it its full name) organises about forty lectures a year. They are aimed at their members, but the public are welcome to attend if they apply in advance for a ticket. The range of subjects is wide, ranging from the likes of 'Architectural Questions Time' and 'Marxism and Red Cadillacs' through to talks on topical political, social or business issues (and there are a couple of lectures each year for children, often on a technological theme). The start time is usually 18.00 – sometimes 14.30 and the venue is usually the Society's impressive lecture theatre. / Tube: Embankment.

St Martin-in-the-Fields WC2

Trafalgar Square   0171-930 1862   2–2C

One of the grandest of London's churches – well, its parish does include Buckingham Palace – and a particularly fine sight when floodlit by night. It was designed by James Gibbs and completed in 1726. There are one hour concerts every weekday (except Thursdays) at 13.05 – a perfect break from one of the most hectic parts of London or a suitable finale to a visit to the neighbouring National Gallery (see also). / Times: 08.00-18.00; Tube: Charing Cross.

Salvation Army International Heritage Centre WC1

117-121 Judd Street   0171-387 1656   4–3C

Discover what inspired William Booth to devote his life to the poor and homeless – the history of the Salvation Army from 1865 is the subject of this exhibition at the Army's King's Cross headquarters. There is a one-hour recorded tour of the exhibition, for which – unusually – there is no charge. / Times: Mon-Fri 09.30-15.30, Sat 09.30-12.30; Tube: King's Cross.

Selfridges W1

400 Oxford Street   0171-629 1234   2–2A

Oxford Street's grand department store has recently completed a major redevelopment programme. Its fine, spacious premises have some quite spectacular displays, and the windows are sometimes very impressive. There is a tourist information office in the basement. / Times: Mon-Sat 09.30-19.00 (Thu 20.00); Tube: Marble Arch, Bond Street.

Sir John Soane's Museum WC2

13 Lincoln's Inn Fields   0171-405 2107   2–1D

One of the most extraordinary houses in the world, built by the great architect between 1812 and 1837, for his own occupation and to house his eclectic collection of treasures. This includes important (and sometimes fascinating) artefacts from Egyptian, Greek and Roman civilisations, and there are also some pictures, most famously Hogarth's series, The Rake's Progress. The greatest attraction, however, is found in wandering around this labyrinthine house, which is quite unlike any other. / Times: Tue-Sat 10.00-17.00, first Tue of month 18.00-21.00; Tube: Holborn.

Sotheby's W1

34-35 New Bond Street   0171-493 8080   2–2B

Sotheby's is possibly the best known of the great international art auctioneers. Details of access are broadly as for their great competitor, Christie's. / Times: *Mon-Fri 09.00-16.30; occasional weekend viewing;* Tube: *Piccadilly Circus, Bond Street.*

Tate Gallery SW1

Millbank   0171-887 8000   2–4C

The Tate occupies a particularly charming building overlooking the Thames. It is really two galleries, combining, as it does, the functions of national galleries of British art (from the sixteenth century) and of international twentieth century art. Most British artists of any repute are represented, and the Blake and Hogarth collections are particularly fine. A recently added wing, the Clore Galleries, houses the enormous Turner Bequest. Great masters of modern art well represented include Francis Bacon, and there are some key works by Picasso. The gallery is re-hung every year. There are tours of different parts of the collection on weekdays at 11.00, 12.00, 14.00 and 15.00; at 15.45 on Sunday, there is a tour of the highlights of the collection. There are lectures at 13.00 (Tue-Sat) and 14.30 (Sun), and afternoons (Wed-Sun) generally see the showing of a film, not always of the esoteric sort in which most museums specialise. Almost all of the Tate's attractions are without charge, with the exception of the three big annual shows. / Times: *Mon-Sat 10.00-17.50, Sun 14.00-17.50;* Tube: *Pimlico.*

Twinings WC2

216 Strand   0171-353 3511   2–2D

Dating from 1706, the shop of the famous tea company claims to be the oldest in London still in its original ownership and still selling the same product. It certainly has a lot of period charm and its compact premises (suitable for small parties only) house a collection illustrating the history of tea and the company's involvement in it. / Times: *Mon-Fri 09.30-16.30;* Tube: *Temple.*

University College Art Collection WC1

Strang Print Room, University College, Gower Street   0171-387 7050   2–1C

Works on paper are the particular strength of this collection of 8,000 items, which also includes paintings and sculpture. There is no permanent exhibition and, to show off the works, a programme of temporary shows is organised. / Times: *Mon-Fri 13.00-14.30 during term time;* Tube: *Warren Street, Goodge Street.*

Wallace Collection W1

Manchester Square   0171-935 0687   2–1A

Hertford House, an imposing mansion just north of Oxford Street, contains one of the most splendid collections of pictures and objets d'art in London. It has been suggested that Gallery 21, with its pictures by Watteau and Fragonard, houses the finest group of French eighteenth century pictures which can be seen in a single room anywhere. The collection also includes works by Rembrandt, Rubens and Hals (The Laughing Cavalier). Extraordinary clocks, Sèvres porcelain and armour are among the other attractions. / Times: *Mon-Sat 10.00-17.00, Sun 14.00-17.00;* Tube: *Bond Street.*

Westminster Abbey * SW1

0171-222 5152   2–3C

There is no other building in England as historic as this great church, whose consecration predated the Invasion of 1066 by a few months, and which has been the setting for every Coronation since. Unfortunately, the strain of accommodating over three million visitors a year means that it can be difficult to find peace in which to appreciate the magnificent architecture (mainly thirteenth to sixteenth centuries) or to explore the numerous tombs and memorials. The cloisters and nave are always – subject to services – open, but there is a charge to visit the Royal Chapels, except on Wednesday evening (18.00-19.45) when you can (as at the time of writing) have the run of the place free of charge. A good way to get some tranquillity whilst admiring the building is to attend the short weekly organ recital at 17.45 on Sundays, or one of the many services (and at evensong, except on Wednesday when it is spoken, you can also appreciate the Abbey's very fine choir).
/ Times: Mon-Fri 09.20-16.00, Sat 09.20-14.00 & 15.45-17.00; Tube: Westminster.

Westminster Cathedral SW1

Ashley Place, Victoria Street   0171-834 7452   2–4C

Completed in 1903, this Byzantine-style Roman Catholic cathedral houses some fine marble-work and mosaics, with the sculptures of the fourteen Stations of the Cross by Eric Gill being particularly renowned. The cathedral is famous for its choir, and services are sung daily except in August. Unfortunately there is a small charge to ascend the 'campanile' (bell tower), which gives a fine view over much of London. / Times: 07.00-20.00; Tube: Victoria.

Outdoor attractions

Bond Street W1

2–2B

If you're seriously into window-shopping, you certainly shouldn't miss the extraordinary row of shops to be found in this street which, for more than three centuries, has been London's most fashionable boutique thoroughfare. All the shops whose very names conjure up wild extravagance are here – Cartier, Tiffany, Versace – to name but three. Most of the best names are in Old Bond Street (the Piccadilly end of the street), but, externally at least, the most impressive shop of all is Asprey of 165 New Bond Street. / Tube: Green Park.

Buckingham Palace * SW1

2–3B
The Queen's house (the principal residence of the Sovereign only since Victoria's day) is one of the few which always advertises whether its principal resident is in – the royal standard then flies from the main flagpole. The main façade, facing the Mall, is much more recent (1913) than the rest of the building and, as is often noted, gives the impression of nothing so much as a more-important-than-usual branch of Barclays Bank. To get a better (and more sympathetic) feeling of what lies behind the façade, walk down Buckingham Gate, and appreciate the side view of the palace. The Queen's private quarters are on the other side, overlooking Constitution Hill. (There is a charge for the recently instituted Summer tours of the interior of the palace, as there is for admission to the Queen's Gallery or the Royal Mews.) One of the best times to visit, of course, is for the Changing of the Guard (see also).
/ Tube: St James's Park, Victoria.

Cleopatra's Needle WC2

Victoria Embankment   2–2D
This 3,500 year old obelisk, now by the side of the Thames, was taken from near the Temple of the Sun God in Heliopolis in Egypt, and was presented to Britain by the Turkish Viceroy in 1819. It has a twin, which stands in New York's Central Park. / Tube: Embankment.

Coram's Fields WC1

93 Guilford Street   0171-837 6138   2–1D
Seven acres of central London to which adults (over 16) are not admitted – unless accompanied by a child! This shady playground – the legacy of an eighteenth century philanthropist – is a boon for harassed parents. It boasts a paddling pool, play equipment, a sports area, a pets corner and a duck pond. / Times: 09.00-20.00 (Easter-end Oct), dusk (Winter); Tube: Russell Square.

Covent Garden WC2

0171-836 9136   2–2C
Covent Garden, with its eighteenth century market-setting and its colourful shops, stalls and cafés, is one of the most agreeable and most popular places for a stroll in central London. There's almost invariably something going on in the way of busking or more serious street-theatre – the Market office (on the number given) can provide information about forthcoming attractions. / Tube: Covent Garden.

Eros SW1

Piccadilly Circus   2–2C
Although invariably known as Eros, the famous, small statue at Piccadilly Circus (the world's first to be made of aluminium) in fact represents the Angel of Christian Charity. The statue looks down the avenue named after Lord Shaftesbury, in whose memory the figure was erected. / Tube: Piccadilly Circus.

Fortnum & Mason Clock W1
181 Piccadilly   2–2B
On the hour, every hour, four feet high figures of Mr Fortnum and Mr Mason emerge from their doors above the shop's main entrance, face each other and bow. An eighteenth century air is then played on seventeen bells. The two gentlemen then bow again and retire to their respective quarters. All in all, it's quite an amusing performance from one of London's few performing clocks. / Tube: *Piccadilly Circus.*

Green Park SW1
0171-930 1793   2–3B
These 53 acres by Piccadilly comprise what the unkind might describe as the Cinderella of the Royal Parks – alone among them, it lacks a lake, it lacks flowers and it lacks summer music. It is, however, a very relaxing place and very central. Constitution Hill (which runs along the park's southern border) is so called in commemoration of Charles II's morning walks in the park. / Times: *24 hours;* Tube: *Green Park, Hyde Park Corner.*

Riverside Walks
See the South section for suggestions of interesting walks by the Thames.

St James's Park SW1
0171-930 1793   2–3C
This is possibly the most beautiful, and certainly the most highly cultivated, of the Royal Parks. Situated as it is in the ceremonial heart of London, between Westminster and Buckingham Palace, it offers idyllic views in both directions. The park (93 acres in extent) was acquired by Henry VIII as the garden for St James's Palace, but owes much of its current appearance to John Nash, whose designs were commissioned in the reign of George IV. During the summer, there are frequent concerts at the band-stand. The pelicans are fed at 15.00 every afternoon. / Times: *24 hours;* Tube: *St James's Park.*

Speakers' Corner W2
Hyde Park (NE corner)   2–2A
For more than a century, this has been the London home of the soapbox orator – Sunday afternoons sees the expression of a whole kaleidoscope of views, from the slightly off-beat to the decidedly cranky. / Tube: *Marble Arch.*

Swiss Centre Clock W1
Leicester Square   2–2C
The Swiss Centre boasts a fine 27-bell glockenspiel, which plays a selection of Alpine and other tunes. Sounding the hour takes about five minutes, during which a procession of cows, sheep, milkmaids, etc makes its way around the base of the clock. There are performances at noon, 18.00, 19.00 and 20.00 every day, and, at weekends on the hour every hour, between noon and 20.00, except 13.00. / Tube: *Piccadilly Circus.*

Trafalgar Square WC2

Trafalgar Square   2–2C

This great, central square, dominated by the National Gallery (see also) is famous for its 170 feet high column dedicated to the memory of Lord Nelson (1843); its fountains and its pigeons. The statues of imperial lions (Landseer, 1867) are also well known, despite the fact that real lions never sit as represented – they always lie on their side. / Tube: *Leicester Square, Charing Cross.*

Victoria Tower Gardens SW1

Millbank   2–4C

This quiet and extremely scenic garden, beneath the looming presence of the Victoria Tower (at the other end of the Houses of Parliament from Big Ben) is graced by a cast of Rodin's Burghers of Calais and by a bronze of the Suffragette, Emmeline Pankhurst. / Times: *07.00-dusk;* Tube: *Westminster.*

West London

Introduction

West London offers a lot of possibilities to those who want to combine a little artistic or intellectual interest (perhaps a visit to the Victoria & Albert Museum, the Serpentine Gallery or the National Sound Archive) with a visit to one of the beautiful green spaces which dot the area, such as Hyde Park, Kensington Gardens and Holland Park.

This combination makes it an excellent area for days out with the kids, for whom the Natural History and Science Museums are top attractions. Both those museums are open free of charge only later on in the day, so it makes sense to do a park first, and to finish up on an educational note.

Away from the centre and its famous parks, the area is rich with fine houses and gardens, such as Osterley Park, Chiswick House and Hampton Court. Take a picnic, and both should, if the weather is fine, provide a good day out. Both of these houses are close by for a Riverside Walk, either for a stroll after lunch or for some more serious exercise. For those who prefer to amble in a more urban, or accessible, environment, the pleasures of Saturday's Portobello Road market are hard to beat.

Some lesser-known central attractions in the area well worth investigating include the Royal Hospital (and the neighbouring Ranelagh Gardens) in Chelsea and Leighton House Museum and Art Gallery in Holland Park. Further out, Pitshanger Manor Museum and Gunnersbury Park Museum both offer interesting and attractive houses to visit, set in pleasant parks.

Chelsea Information Office SW3
Old Town Hall, King's Road   0171-352 1856   3–3C
Chelsea's information office is in the same building as a good reference library. / Times: Mon-Fri 09.00-13.00, 14.00-17.00 (Fri 16.45); Tube: Sloane Square.

Hillingdon Tourist Information Centre, Middx
Central Library, High St, Uxbridge   01895-250706   off map
/ Times: Mon, Tue, Thu 09.30-20.00; Wed, Fri 09.30-17.30; Sat 09.30-16.00; Tube: Uxbridge.

Hounslow Tourist Information Centre, Middx
24 Treaty Centre, Hounslow   0181-572 8279   off map
/ Times: Mon-Sat 09.30-17.30 (Tue & Thu 20.00); Tube: Hounslow Central.

Twickenham Tourist Information Centre, Middlesex
Civic Centre, York St, Twickenham   0181-891 7272   off map
/ Times: Mon-Fri 09.00-17.15 (17.00 Fri); Brit Rail: Twickenham.

Indoor attractions

Chelsea Football Club, SW6
Fulham Road   0171-385 0710   3–4B
If you, your kids or your spouse are Chelsea fans, and you would like to arrange to see behind the scenes at Stamford Bridge, then the club is generally happy to oblige. Requests should be made to 'Chelsea in the Community' at the number above.
/ *Tube:* Fulham Broadway.

Goethe Institute SW7
50 Princes Gate, Exhibition Road   0171-411 3400   3–1C
The institute has a small gallery which has changing exhibitions of works by artists from Germany or those connected in some other way with the country. / *Times:* Mon-Fri 10.00-20.00 (Fri 16.00), Sat 09.30-12.30; *Tube:* South Kensington.

Gunnersbury Park Museum W3
Gunnersbury Park, Pope's Lane   0181-992 1612   1–3A
This very grand local museum (housed in a former Rothschild family house, built in 1835 on the site of a former royal residence) houses a large collection on the history of Ealing and Hounslow. It benefits from an extremely pleasant park location. There are occasional exhibitions, not always of purely local interest.
/ *Times:* Mon-Fri 13.00-17.00, Sat, Sun & Bank Hols 13.00-18.00 (Apr-Oct); 13.00-16.00 (Nov-Mar); *Tube:* Acton Town.

Heathrow Airport, Middx
Hounslow   0181-745 5259   off map
Heathrow is staggering in terms of the scale of its operations. It handles nearly 50,000,000 passengers (ie almost the same as the population of the UK) annually, and deals with more international passengers than any other airport in the world. There is a viewing area in Terminal 2, from which you can watch all the comings and goings. A helpful brochure is provided, which explains the functions of the various buildings and contains a plane-spotter's guide to tail markings, so you can identify the various airlines. If you want to make sure you catch a Concorde (so to speak) call British Airways on 0181-759 5511 for information on take-off and landing times. (For further inspiration or information while you're at the airport, you can visit the London Tourist Board office on the Underground (Terminals 1,2,3) concourse.) / *Times:* 09.00-30 mins before dusk; *Tube:* Heathrow Terminals 1,2,3.

Hogarth's House W4
Hogarth Lane, Great West Road   0181-994 6757   1–3A
Ironically (given that it's just off the Great West Road), the great English engraver and painter William Hogarth (1697-1764) apparently chose this pretty Chiswick house as his home because of its quiet location. Apart from some memorabilia associated with the artist, the main attractions are some of his most famous series of engravings (such as Marriage à la Mode and Industry and Idleness) and the attractive garden, which contains a mulberry tree dating from the painter's time. / *Times:* Mon & Wed-Sat 11.00-18.00, Sun 14.00-18.00 (Apr-Sep); Mon & Wed-Sat 11.00-16.00, Sun 14.00-16.00 (Oct-Mar); *Tube:* Turnham Green.

Leighton House Museum and Art Gallery W14

12 Holland Park Road   0171-602 3316   1–3B

No visitor to Holland Park should miss this extraordinary mid-Victorian house, with later Moorish Hall (complete with small pool). It is a wonderful setting for the permanent collection of paintings by Lord Leighton (1803-96) and some of his contemporaries; in summer, the garden (which contains some sculptures) is open. There are also temporary exhibitions in the recently refurbished Perrin Gallery – if you want to assess current standards in what was once London's most famous artistic quarter, don't miss the Kensington and Chelsea Artist's Show in February (1995) or October (1996).
/ Times: 11.00-17.30 Mon-Sat; Tube: High Street Kensington.

National Army Museum SW3

Royal Hospital Road   0171-730 0717   3–3D

The Army's own museum relates its history, from the raising of the Yeomen of the Guard in 1485 all the way through to involvement in contemporary UN peacekeeping operations. There is a major collection of uniforms, as well as paintings of famous battle scenes, portraits by Reynolds and Gainsborough, and displays of weaponry and medals. A visit here makes a good fit with one to the neighbouring Royal Hospital (see also). / Times: 10.00-17.30; Tube: Sloane Square.

National Sound Archive SW7

29 Exhibition Road   0171-412 7430   3–1C

One of the largest sound archives in the world, the audio sub-division of the British Library has huge holdings of musical and other sound recordings (including drama, wildlife and BBC material). The sound collection is not really "browsable", however, and to listen to any particular item, an appointment must be made several days ahead. A visitor centre opens in early 1995. / Times: Mon-Fri 10.00-17.00 (21.00 Thu); Tube: South Kensington.

Natural History Museum * SW7

Cromwell Road   0171-938 9123   3–2C

Free time is short at this famous museum – at weekends, indeed, you get only 50 minutes, so may we suggest a few of the key attractions. You will want to spend a few minutes in the cathedral-like central hall, dominated by the skeleton of Diplodocus, one of the largest creatures which ever lived. In the remaining time, you might like to take in the Dinosaurs exhibition in the new Ronson Gallery, or you might prefer to find out how you yourself work, by visiting the Human Biology Gallery. The museum has many interactive displays – it even offers the possibility of inter-acting with an earthquake.
/ Times: Mon-Fri 16.30-17.50; Sat, Sun & Bank Hols 17.00-17.50; Tube: South Kensington.

The Orangery and the Ice House W8

Holland Park   0171-603 1123   3–1A

The charming eighteenth century glasshouse in the centre of Holland Park, and the nearby Ice House are both used for high quality arts and crafts exhibitions in various media. / Times: 11.00-19.00 (during exhibitions); Tube: High Street Kensington, Holland Park.

Orleans House Gallery, Middx
Riverside, Twickenham   0181-892 0221   off map
Twickenham benefits from an unusually attractive gallery in which to display its borough art collection and in which to hold temporary exhibitions. It was designed by James Gibbs in 1720, as the garden pavilion of a very grand house (demolished in the 1920s) and is richly decorated with ornamental mouldings and gilt. The setting, in a picturesque, riverside, woodland garden (open daylight hours) is a good place for a picnic or as a starting point for a stroll along the Thames. / Times: *Tue-Sat 13.00-17.30 (winter 16.30), Sun & Bank Hols 14.00-17.30 (winter 16.30);* Tube: *Richmond.*

Pitshanger Manor Museum W5
Mattock Lane, Ealing   0181-567 1227   1–2A
This Ealing house, set in a park, already had the benefit of some exquisite plaster work designed by George Dance in the mid eighteenth century, when it attracted the attentions of the great neo-classical architect, Sir John Soane. Between 1800 and 1810, the latter turned the house into a Regency villa for the pleasure of himself and his family. The building (Grade I listed, and open to the public only since 1987) merits a visit in its own right, but there is also a changing display of Martinware – the pottery made by the Martin brothers of Southall between 1877 and 1923.
/ Times: *Tue-Sat 10.00-17.00;* Tube: *Ealing Broadway.*

Polish Institute and Sikorski Museum SW7
20 Princes Gate   0171-589 9249   3–1C
Anyone with even a passing interest in Poland, or in military history, should visit this elegant museum near Hyde Park – it is by far the most important collection of Polish material anywhere outside the country. There are important mementoes of the many conflicts in which Poles have been involved – for example the national flag flown over the ruins of the monastery of Monte Cassino in 1944.
/ Times: *Mon-Fri 14.00-16.00, first Sat of month 10.00-16.00;* Tube: *South Kensington, Knightsbridge.*

Queen's Park Rangers FC W12
South Africa Road   0181-548 2707   –
If you are a Ranger's fan, interested in the idea of a look around Loftus Road then, time permitting, the club will organise a tour for you. Call their "Development" office at the number above. / Tube: *Shepherd's Bush.*

Royal College of Art * SW7
Kensington Gore   0171-584 5020   3–1B
The College is the only exclusively post-graduate art school in Europe – it has courses in almost all art-forms, but is particularly well known for fashion. They have a large amount of gallery space. This is used for regular "Work in progress" exhibitions, and, in May and June, Degree shows – for all of these there is no charge. The galleries are frequently hired by outsiders, and many of those shows are also free.
/ Times: *During exhibitions: Mon-Fri 10.00-18.00;* Tube: *Knightsbridge, South Kensington.*

The mobile phone • For everyday • For everyone

Royal Hospital SW3

Royal Hospital Road   0171-730 5282   3–3D

Wren's elegant 1682 building, founded by Charles II for veteran soldiers, remains the home of the Chelsea Pensioners, who can sometimes be spotted around the area wearing their splendid scarlet uniforms. The Great Hall, the Chapel and the Museum may be visited. Don't miss the lovely grounds (Ranelagh Gardens – see also). / *Times:* Mon-Sat 10.00-12.00, 14.00-16.00; Sun (Hall & Chapel only) 14.00-16.00; *Tube:* Sloane Square.

Science Museum * SW7

Exhibition Road   0171-938 8080/8008   3–1C

Appropriately for the prime technological museum of the first industrial nation, the exhibits here contain many "firsts": the first steam engine of the eighteenth century and the first steam turbine of the nineteenth, Stephenson's train (the "Rocket") and the Vickers Vimy aircraft which made the first non-stop Atlantic crossing in 1919. Many attractions are more contemporary, including the Apollo 10 spacecraft, still scorched from re-entry into the atmosphere. There's always a great deal going on throughout the museum, and there are enough "hands-on" exhibits in the 40 galleries to keep the most fidgety children happy. / *Times:* 16.30-18.00; *Tube:* South Kensington.

Serpentine Gallery W2

Kensington Gardens   0171-402 0343   3–1C

A number of modern and contemporary exhibitions are held every year in this airy gallery, which benefits from one of the most charming locations in London. There are usually talks by artists and critics on Sunday afternoons at 15.00. / *Times:* 10.00-18.00 (during exhibitions); *Tube:* Lancaster Gate.

Victoria & Albert Museum * SW7

Cromwell Road   0171-938 8500   3–2C

The V&A holds the world's greatest collection of decorative art and design. Ceramics, furniture and dress are but three examples of the fields in which it holds comprehensive selections, and the museum is also home to the national collections of photography and watercolours. Major new galleries are devoted to European, Japanese, Chinese and Indian art, and to the architect Frank Lloyd Wright. The size of the collection is such that it's a good idea to start off with one of the guided tours at 11.00, 12.00, 14.00 or 15.00 (Mon 12.15, 14.00 or15.00). During the school holidays, there are even occasional tours for children (as well as activities designed to appeal to all the family). There are always a number of exhibitions in progress. They are generally without charge, except for the major temporary exhibition of the moment. Entrance to the museum is free, and if you decline to make a contribution you will still be admitted. It should be noted, however, that – much more so than is generally the case – there is a strongly "suggested" level of voluntary donation (about a fiver). / *Times:* Mon 12.00-17.50, Tue-Sun 10.00-17.50; *Tube:* South Kensington.

obello Road Market W10, W11

aturday, Portobello market is undoubtedly the place in West
on for combining people-watching and browsing. The street
et stretches for over a mile, and in fact comprises several
rent markets. The most famous, the antiques market, is at the
end, but there is also a food market, bric-à-brac stalls and
er the Westway) a good gathering of vendors of trendy clothing
accessories. / *Tube:* Notting Hill Gate, Ladbroke Grove.

elagh Gardens SW3

al Hospital Road   3–3D
rt from when they are cordoned off every year for the famous
sea Flower Show (in May), these well kept gardens lead a rather
profile life. They are, however, unusually pretty and intimate. A
here combines very well with one to the neighbouring Royal
pital (see also). / *Times:* 10.00 (Sun 14.00)–30 mins before dusk, but
ed 13.00-14.00; *Tube:* Sloane Square.

erside Walks

e the South section for suggestions of interesting walks by the
ames.

islip Woods, Middx

islip   01895 250635   off map
ese 700 acres include, in the 250 acre Park Wood, the largest
broken area of woodland in London. A particular attraction of the
yhurst Wood Country Park, which forms another part of the
oods, is its barbecue sites – although there is a charge to book
ese, you don't have to pay if you are prepared to take "pot luck" –
d there are also picnic sites. "A short guide to Ruislip Woods" is
vailable in local libraries or write to Recreation Unit, Local Services,
vic Centre, Uxbridge, Middx UB8 1UW. / *Brit Rail:* Ruislip (then H13,
n 114 bus).

William Morris Society W6

Kelmscott House, 26 Upper Mall   0181-741 3735   1–3A
*Occupying part of the house in which Morris – socialist, designer and
author – lived from 1878 until his death in 1896, this small
collection of memorabilia, designs and books includes one of the
original presses upon which his novels, poetry and pamphlets were
printed. Devotees should also see the entry for the William Morris
Gallery in the East End.* / *Times:* Thu & Sat 14.00-17.00;
Tube: Hammersmith.

Outdoor attractions

Burnham Beeches, Bucks

Farnham Common   01753-647358   off map
*Though not quite IN London, this famous beauty spot – one of the
finest examples of ancient woodland in Britain – can fairly claim to
be OF the capital city as it has been owned by the City Corporation
for more than a century. The most famous feature of the 540 acre
site is the beech pollards, some of which are almost half a
millennium old. Given the wood's accessibility (just north of Junction 6
of the M4), it would be the perfect place to get away from it all if it
were not for the fact that every year half a million other people have
the same idea too! Autumn is the very best time to visit.*
/ *Times:* Pedestrians 24 hours, vehicles 08.00- one hour after sunset;
Brit Rail: Slough (then bus to Farnham Common).

Bushy Park, Middx

0181-979 1586   off map
*This park is part of Wren's grand design for neighbouring Hampton
Court Park and boasts a fine chestnut avenue. Herds of red and
fallow deer roam its 1100 acres. The Woodland Gardens, with their
fine azaleas, camellias and rhododendrons, are a post-war addition.*
/ *Times:* Pedestrians, 24 hours; vehicles 6.30-00.00; *Brit Rail:* Hampton Wick.

Chelsea Harbour SW10

0171-351 4433   3–4B
*This contemporary riverside development never seems to have lived
up to its aspirations, but it does offer quite an attractive marina, a
pleasant place for a riverside walk on a sunny day, and some good
views. Given its relatively central location, it has a surprisingly far
away feel.* / *Tube:* Earl's Court (then C3 bus).

Chiswick House W4

Burlington Lane   0181-995 5390   1–3A
*The mainly wooded, 64 acre gardens of this fine neo-classical villa
have suitably Italianate highlights – statues, temples, urns and
obelisks – and there is also a lake. The information centre (which
has a small exhibition about the history of the garden) can equip you
with a park trails pamphlet and map. There is a picnic area (and
also a café). The house, to which there is an entry charge, is run by
the National Trust.* / *Times:* 08.00-dusk; *Tube:* Turnham Green (then E3 bus).

Crane Park Island, Middx

Crane Park, Twickenham   0181-898 9582   off map

This small island (just over 4 acres), reached by bridge, has its place in history – the old gunpowder mill here (now demolished) is believed to have been where Guy Fawkes obtained his supplies. Nowadays, its attractions are rather more peaceful, and it's an agreeable site, run by the London Wildlife Trust. There are three paths, one of which (Hobbin Path) is suitable for disabled people. / Times: *dawn-dusk;* Brit Rail: *Witton.*

Gunnersbury Triangle Nature Reserve W4

Chiswick   1–3A

This six acre site developed a rich covering of vegetation after being surrounded by railway tracks in the late nineteenth century. It has been undisturbed, apart from some allotments, ever since. It was threatened by development in the early 1980s and became a "test case". The conservationists won, and this was the first time that a planning inspector had preferred nature conservation to development on a city site. It is now managed by the London Wildlife Trust. The reserve is open Sunday only at the time of writing – check with the Trust (tel 0171-278 6612) for further information. /* Tube: *Chiswick Park.*

Hampton Court Palace *, Middx

0181-781 9500   off map

Both the wonderful garden and the park of Wolsey's great riverside palace (completed by Henry VIII and substantially altered by William and Mary) are open to the public without charge. The formal gardens are the most visited free attraction of their type in the country, and include features from Victorian times, as well as from the earlier periods of the palace's construction. Around the gardens, in the 560 acre park, graze the descendants of the deer hunted by the Tudor monarchs. The Great Vine, planted by Capability Brown in 1768, is claimed to be the oldest in the world, and still bears fruit. There is a charge for access to the palace and the maze. /* Times: *07.00-21.00 (dusk if earlier), 365 days a year;* Brit Rail: *Hampton Court.*

Holland Park W8

Ilchester Place   0171-603 2129   3–1A

Until some 40 years ago, Holland Park was an extraordinary hangover from former days – a private "country" estate, in the middle of London. It maintains a unique and charming character, and, in spite of its relatively small size (54 acres), some of it is heavily wooded (and managed so as to enhance wildlife). It is one of the most attractive parks in London. Apart from its superb formal gardens, it benefits from a recent addition in the form of the Kyoto Garden, installed by Japanese benefactors in 1991. Other attractions include a large play-park and the Ecology Centre, which has a series of free talks and events. The park contains the Orangery and the Ice House (see also). / Times: *07.30-30 mins before dusk;* Tube: *Holland Park, Kensington High Street.*

Hyde Park W2

0171-298 2000   3–1C

The greatest of the central Royal Parks was origin⸱⸱ Henry VIII from the Abbey at Westminster as a pr⸱⸱ ground. Its 340 acres now offer a variety of attract⸱⸱ the formal gardens along its south side, to Rotten R⸱⸱ for more than 300 years), a river (the Serpentine)⸱⸱ woods and grass, designed to look like an idealised⸱⸱ England. In the summer, there are concerts at the b⸱⸱ (afternoons and evenings on Sundays and Bank Holi⸱⸱ Corner (see also) is situated in the north east corner⸱⸱ Kensington Gardens (effectively the continuation of H⸱⸱ west) also has its own entry. / Times: *05.00-00.00;* Tube:⸱⸱ Hyde Park Corner, Marble Arch, Lancaster Gate, Queensway.*

Kensington Gardens W8

0171-298 2100   3–1B

These were the private gardens of Kensington Palace⸱⸱ designed by Wren) and were largely laid out under the⸱⸱ Queen Caroline. The gardens were opened to the public⸱⸱ Victoria and are now effectively an extension of Hyde P⸱⸱ Attractions in the 275 acres include the Boating Pond (⸱⸱ only, please), the charming small statue of Peter Pan an⸱⸱ pretty area in the immediate vicinity of the palace itself.⸱⸱ also house the Serpentine Gallery (see also) and the High⸱⸱ standing Scaffolding in the World (formerly known as the⸱⸱ Memorial). In summer, there are weekly concerts at the⸱⸱ / Times: *Dawn-dusk;* Tube: *Bayswater, Lancaster Gate, Queensway, H⸱⸱ Kensington.*

Marble Hill House *, Middx

Richmond Road, Twickenham   0181-892 5115   off m⸱⸱

Built in the 1720s as a retreat from court life for Henrietta⸱⸱ Countess of Suffolk (George II's mistress), this Palladian vill⸱⸱ the most perfect surviving examples of the type – inhabits a⸱⸱ park which stretches down to the river. The central attractio⸱⸱ house is the Great Room, with its gilded carving and painting⸱⸱ Ancient Rome by Panini. A charge is being introduced for adr⸱⸱ to the house (but not the gardens) in April 1995. / Times: *10.0⸱⸱ (Apr-Oct); Wed-Sun 10.00-16.00 (Nov-Mar);* Tube: *Richmond.*

Osterley Park *, Middx

Isleworth   0181-560 3918   off map

This is one of the last great houses with an intact estate in Gre⸱⸱ London, set in 140 acres of landscaped park with ornamental l⸱⸱ Originally a sixteenth century mansion (built for Sir Thomas⸱⸱ Gresham, founder of the Royal Exchange), it was transformed i⸱⸱ neo-classical style by Robert Adam in the eighteenth century. It's⸱⸱ been a National Trust property for over half a century, but they⸱⸱ took over the management five years ago and are now in the⸱⸱ process of restoring the garden to the appearance it would have⸱⸱ two centuries ago. There is a charge for admission to the house a⸱⸱ for car parking. / Times: *Park: 06.30-19.30 or sunset if earlier;* Tube: *Osterl⸱⸱*

North London

Introduction

North London's unique strength is the way it contains pockets of real nature, which seem to be only a stone's throw from the metropolis itself. The most obvious example is Hampstead Heath, but there is also Highgate Wood, and both are within a few tube-stops of anywhere in central London.

In addition, much of North London is provided with fine parks. It has its own ornamental Royal Park, in the form of Regent's Park; its extension, Primrose Hill has exceptional views and the northerly Alexandra Palace Park gives yet another fine perspective on the city below. The grounds of Golder's Green Crematorium are a fine amenity, relatively unknown to those outside the locality.

Few would dispute that Hampstead is the by far the finest village in London, and two of its lovely period houses may be visited – Burgh House (whose museum gives the history of the area) and Keats House. The village's grandest residence, Kenwood House, at the top of the Heath, has an excellent period art collection.

In a very different idiom, St John's Wood's Saatchi Gallery brings some of the most challenging contemporary art before the public.

For people who like being among people, the undoubted attraction here is Camden Market

For children, it's probably the green spaces and the nature which are the main plus point. For the more inquisitive, however, the Wellcome Galleries, with their interactive displays, should not be overlooked.

Harrow Tourist Information Centre, Middx
Civic Centre, Station Rd, Harrow   0181-424 1103   off map
/ *Times:* Mon-Fri 09.00-17.00; *Brit Rail:* Harrow & Wealdstone.

Islington Visitor Information Centre N1
44 Duncan Street   0171-278 8787   4–3D
/ *Times:* Mon-Sat 10.00-5.00; *Tube:* Angel.

The mobile phone • For everyday • For everyone

Indoor attractions

Bruce Castle Museum N17
Lordship Lane   0181-808 8772   off map
*Haringey's local museum occupies an elegant and striking Tudor
house. It has been in use as such since the beginning of the century
and has a wide collection of items of local interest, from the
Highgate Roman kiln through to Victorian costumes. There is also a
postal history collection, reflecting the one-time residence of Roland
Hill, the inventor of the penny post. Temporary art exhibitions are
held from time to time. During the summer, they offer regular arts
and crafts activities. / Times: Wed-Sun 13.00-17.00; Tube: Wood Green (then
243 bus).*

Burgh House NW3
New End Square   0171-431 0144   4–1A
*This extremely handsome Queen Anne house (1703), is well worth a
visit for its architecture, for its pictures and for its creaking charm.
There are displays about the history of Hampstead (which has long
been regarded as one of the most salubrious places to live in or near
the capital) and changing exhibitions on the history of the area. The
house makes an ideal stopping-off point between the tube station
and the Heath. / Times: Wed-Sun (and Bank Hols) 12.00-17.00;
Tube: Hampstead.*

Camden Arts Centre NW3
Arkwright Road   0171-435 2643   4–2A
*The centre's three galleries hold about half a dozen contemporary
art exhibitions a year. During shows, there are usually Sunday talks
every two to three weeks. / Times: Thu-Sun 12.00-8.00, Fri-Sun 12.00-18.00;
Tube: Finchley Road.*

Church Farmhouse Museum NW4
Greyhound Hill   0181-203 0130   off map
*Built in 1660, this charming building (the oldest thereabouts), set in
a small garden, combines displays of nineteenth century life – a
period dining room, scullery and kitchen – with changing exhibitions
about local and social history and decorative arts and crafts.
/ Times: Mon-Thu 10.00-17.00, Sat 10.00-13.00 & 14.00-17.30, Sun 14.00-17.30;
Tube: Hendon Central.*

Crafts Council N1
44a Pentonville Road   0171-278 7700   4–3D
*The Council is the national body for promoting contemporary crafts,
such as pottery, textiles and printing. Its premises include a picture
library and reference library as well as a gallery. There are five major
exhibitions a year – either retrospectives of major makers or
thematic shows of contemporary craft. There is a general information
service relating to contemporary British crafts, available by phone,
letter or visiting. / Times: Tue-Sat 11.00-18.00, Sun 14.00-18.00; Tube: Angel.*

Forty Hall, Middx

Forty Hill, Enfield   0181-363 8196   off map

Forty Hall was first built in 1629 (the date is given in the ceiling of one of the first floor rooms). It has since had a chequered history and has been owned by many families (the last being the Parker Bowles family who lived there until the '40s). Its particular attraction is the richness and diversity of the interiors added at different points over the years. In use as a museum for the last four decades, it now houses a display on local history, a popular children's gallery, and an exhibition devoted to advertising and packaging.
/ *Times:* Thu-Sun 11.00-17.00; *Tube:* Enfield Town (then 191, 231 bus).

Glasshouse N1

21 St Albans Place   0171-359 8162   4–3D

You are welcome to stop by at this Islington glass-blowing workshop, where you can watch intricate glass artefacts being blown and formed. There's also a gallery, where you can see some very impressive examples of the modern glass-blower's art.
/ *Times:* 10.00-18.00 Tue-Sat (gallery only, Sat); *Tube:* Angel.

Grange Museum of Community History NW10

Neasden Lane   0181-452 8311   1–1A

Brent's community museum, in a converted eighteenth century stable-block, includes an Edwardian draper's shop (transplanted from Willesden High Road) and a Victorian Parlour. A permanent exhibition, The Brent People, includes a computerised database of local photographs. This is a "child-friendly" museum, with a large play area and an enclosed garden (with Victorian herb border) open for picnicking. / *Times:* Tue-Fri 11.00-17.00, Sat 10.00-17.00, Sun 14.00-17.00 (Jun-Aug); Mon-Fri 11.00-17.00, Sat 10.00-17.00 (Sep-May); *Tube:* Neasden.

Harrow Museum and Heritage Centre, Middx

Headstone Manor, Pinner View   0181-861 2626   off map

Originally built for the Archbishops of Canterbury in the fourteenth century, this moated manor house (Grade I listed) has '30s interiors which are still in the course of renovation. It benefits from a pretty setting in a park, and there is also a large and interesting tithe barn (where a Victorian room-setting and changing exhibitions are displayed). / *Times:* Wed-Sun 12.30 (Sat, Sun 10.30)-17.00, Bank Hols 10.30-17.00; *Tube:* Harrow on the Hill (then H14 or H15).

Harrow School Old Speech Room Gallery, Middx

Church Hill, Harrow on the Hill   0181-869 1205   off map

This famous old school has accumulated a number of treasures over the years, and the principal ones are kept on show in their gallery. There are some important antiquities, and fine collections of ancient books and nineteenth century watercolours. Works by old Harrovians (of Venice, by Sir Winston Churchill, for example) and of former pupils (such as Lord Byron) complete the collection. / *Times:* Term, 14.30-17.00 (ex Wed); hols, Mon-Fri 14.15-17.00; *Tube:* Harrow on the Hill (then 258 bus).

Islington Museum Gallery N1
268 Upper Street, Islington   0171-354 9442   4–2D
It is surprising that Islington lacks a fully-fledged local museum. They have started to remedy the position, though, and it is hoped that this "museum gallery" – which stages temporary exhibitions relating to the area – is the precursor to a more permanent and comprehensive venture. / Times: Wed-Fri 11.00-15.00, Sat 10.00-17.00, Sun 14.00-16.00; Tube: Highbury & Islington.

Keats House NW3
Keats Grove   0171-435 2062   4–1A
The great poet spent most of his working life in this Hampstead house (consisting of two very pretty Regency cottages), which contains memorabilia of Keats and his family. / Times: 10.00-13.00 (not Sun), 14.00-18.00 (17.00, Sat & Sun) (Apr-Oct); 13.00 (Sat & Sun 14.00)-17.00 & also Sat 10.00-13.00 (Nov-Mar); Tube: Hampstead.

Kenwood House NW3
Hampstead Lane   0181-348 1286   4–1A
Perching like a grand wedding cake above Hampstead Heath, this neo-classical house (with Robert Adam façade, 1760s) provides a great cultural climax to a visit to the heath. The house (which was bequeathed to the nation by the first Earl of Iveagh in 1927) is certainly worth a view (the library is reckoned as one of Adam's finest rooms), as are the artistic treasures within, which include a Rembrandt self-portrait and Vermeer's Guitar Player. / Times: 10.00-18.00 (Apr-Sep); 10.00-16.00 (Oct-Mar); Tube: Archway or Golders Green (then 210 bus).

Lauderdale House Community Arts Centre N6
Waterlow Park, Highgate Hill   0181-348 8716   1–1C
The two galleries of the important house in the centre of the attractive Waterlow Park hold frequently changing exhibitions. / Times: Tue-Fri 11.00-16.00; Tube: Archway (then 143, 210 or 271 bus).

National Museum of Cartoon Art NW1
183 Eversholt Street   0171-388 4326   4–3C
The museum holds changing exhibitions of the best in British and international cartoons, caricatures and comic strips. Entry is free of charge, but a donation is strongly suggested. A change of location is scheduled for early 1995, so ring before setting off. / Times: Mon-Fri 12.00-18.00 (Thu 19.00); Tube: Euston, Euston Square, Warren Street.

Saatchi Collection * NW8
98A Boundary Road   0171-624 8299   4–3A
This white "space" in St John's Wood affords a very striking setting in which to display a changing selection of items from advertising magnate Charles Saatchi's collection of modern art, which is almost certainly the finest of its type in the UK. / Times: Thu 12.00-18.00; Tube: St John's Wood.

Union Chapel N1
Compton Terrace   0171-359 4019   4–2D
The Father Willis organ of this Congregationalist chapel has been little touched since its installation soon after the construction of the chapel in 1897. There are periodic recitals, usually on Saturday evenings. / Tube: Highbury & Islington.

Wellcome Building NW1
183 Euston Road   0171-611 8727   4–4C
There are two interesting attractions in the Wellcome Trust's august HQ building, near Euston. Science for Life is a permanent exhibition, featuring a wide range of displays, many of which benefit from the application of the latest interactive technology – it includes a human cell, magnified a million times, through which you can walk. The History of Medicine gallery principally draws on the huge collection of the Wellcome Institute Library. / Times: Mon-Fri 09.45-17.45, Sat 09.45-13.00; Tube: Euston, Euston Square, Warren Street.

Outdoor attractions

Abney Park Cemetery N16
Stoke Newington High Street   0171-275 9443   1–1C
A surprisingly country-like place (it was originally laid out as an arboretum), this cemetery took over (around 1840) from Bunhill Fields as the final resting place of London's dissenters and non-conformists. General Booth, founder of the Salvation Army, is among those interred here. The main entrance has recently been restored and there is a visitor centre. / Times: 09.00-19.00 (summer); 09.00-15.00 (winter); Brit Rail: Stoke Newington.

Alexandra Palace N22
Alexandra Palace Way   0181-365 2121   off map
This 200 acre North London park is made rather special by its panoramic views over the metropolis as well as its historical associations, as the site of the world's first television studio. The popular "Grove Shows" have been running for a decade – live music every summer Sunday afternoon and, in August, Thursday afternoon shows for the kids as well. Permanent attractions include a children's playground, an animal area (with llama, pony, donkeys and deer) and a conservation area (near the Wood Green entrance). / Times: 24 hours; Tube: Wood Green (then W3 bus).

Camden Lock NW1
0171-284 2084   4–2B
Occupying renovated warehouses, this is arguably the more 'grown up' part of Camden Market. Fashions, jewellery, books, antiques – are amongst the enormous variety of things from the stalls and shops. The lock is open all week, but, as with the rest of the market, Saturdays and Sundays are the peak time for a visit. There are frequent summer attractions (generally during the week), such as street theatre, music and art shows. / Times: 09.30-18.00; Tube: Camden Town, Chalk Farm.

Camden Market NW1
Camden High Street (and surrounding area)   4–2B
At the weekend, the whole of hip young London seems to descend on Camden for its markets – together with the tourists, they make it one of the most visited attractions in town. By no means are prices particularly bargain basement, though, and unless you are shopping for the latest in "wicked" style, the real point of the trip is to stroll around window-shopping and people-watching.
/ *Times: Thu-Sun 09.00-17.00; Tube: Camden Town.*

Camley Street Natural Park NW1
12 Camley Street   0171-833 2311   4–3C
In the inhospitable area north of King's Cross, this tiny (2 acre) site offers an oasis. They cram an amazing amount in – there's a pond, a wood and a marsh, as well as some formal flower-beds. You can obtain information about the London Wildlife Trust (which maintains over 50 nature reserves, of varying sizes, within the London area) from the visitor centre. / Times: Mon-Thu 09.00-17.00, Sat & Sun 11.00-17.00 (summer), 10.00-16.00 (winter); Tube: King's Cross.

Coldfall Wood N10
Crichton Avenue   0181-348 6005   off map
These 35 acres of ancient woodland to the north of Muswell Hill are of great ecological interest. If you intend to explore, call the Conservation Officer who can provide you with a leaflet, "Historic Woodlands in Haringey". Examples of the returning fashion for traditional coppice management may be seen. / Tube: East Finchley.

Finsbury Park N4
0181-808 2625   4–1D
A large part of the 115 acres of this Victorian park is taken up with various sports facilities (for which there is generally a charge), so there's often a lot of activity. You can even go fishing – you do need to obtain a licence, but it's free. Among the other attractions are several children's playgrounds and a conservatory. / Times: 06.30-dusk; Tube: Manor House, Finsbury Park.

Freightliners Farm N7
Sherringham Road   0171-609 0467   4–2D
This 3 1/2 acre city farm in Islington has been going for 20 years, making it the oldest in London. They have all the usual farm animals. A less common attraction is a recently installed sensory garden for disabled people. Stables are opening in spring 1995.
/ *Times: Tue-Sun 9.30-13.00 & 14.00-16.30; Tube: Highbury & Islington.*

Fryent Country Park NW9
Fryent Way   0181-900 5653   1–1A
For those in search of real country in the town, the 260 acres of unspoilt rural farmland here, sandwiched between Wembley and Kingsbury, are pretty much the perfect answer. Nature walks, ponds and a wildlife area are among the attractions. / Times: 24 hours; Tube: Kingsbury, Wembley Park.

Gladstone Park NW10

Dollis Hill Lane   0181-900 5653   1–1A

William Gladstone was a frequent visitor to the fine house (1824) which forms the centrepiece of this very varied 90 acre park between Neasden and Willesden. Other attractions include an arboretum filled with hundreds of exotic trees from all over the world, a pond with ducks and geese, and an old walled garden.
/ Times: *08.00-dusk;* Tube: *Neasden, Dollis Hill.*

Golder's Green Crematorium NW11

Hoop Lane   0181-455 2374   1–1B

The first crematorium in London, founded in 1902, has unusual northern Italianate architecture (by Sir Ernest George, RA, who also designed Claridge's Hotel) and benefits from a beautiful setting in a 12 acre ornamental garden. Those who have been cremated here include Marc Bolan, Joyce Grenfell, Gustave Holst, Charles Rennie Mackintosh and Siegmund Freud. / Times: *09.00-19.00 (winter 17.00);* Tube: *Golders Green.*

Hampstead and Highgate Ponds NW3

Hampstead Heath   0181-348 9945/0171-485 4491   4–1A

Hampstead Heath boasts no fewer than three places to go for a swim. During the season (from 30 April to 18 September) you can choose between the Hampstead Pond (which is mixed), the Highgate Pond (men only – nude bathing is traditional) and the Kenwood Pond (women only). Rather curiously, the last is the most restrictive, with one rule limiting children to those aged 8 and over and only one per adult. Swimmers who do not appear to be "competent" may be asked to leave. The pools are not very well signposted, so don't forget your map. / Times: *Summer: Mixed 10.00-19.00, single sex 07.00-21.00; ring to check winter times;* Tube: *Hampstead, Kentish Town (thenC2 bus).*

Hampstead Heath NW3

0181-348 9945/0171-485 4491   4–1A

Hampstead Heath's 791 acres, presided over by the City Corporation, offer everything from a fine 18th century house and art collection with formal gardens – Kenwood (see also) – to heathland which is as close as you will get to real countryside near central London. There are also tremendous vistas, and the views of the metropolis from some parts of the heath are so fine that they have special legal protection. Other attractions of the heath include the bathing pools (see Hampstead and Highgate Ponds).
/ Times: *24 hours;* Tube: *Hampstead, Golders Green.*

William Morris Society W6
Kelmscott House, 26 Upper Mall   0181-741 3735   1–3A
Occupying part of the house in which Morris – socialist, designer and author – lived from 1878 until his death in 1896, this small collection of memorabilia, designs and books includes one of the original presses upon which his novels, poetry and pamphlets were printed. Devotees should also see the entry for the William Morris Gallery in the East End. / Times: *Thu & Sat 14.00-17.00;* Tube: *Hammersmith.*

Outdoor attractions

Burnham Beeches, Bucks
Farnham Common   01753-647358   off map
Though not quite IN London, this famous beauty spot – one of the finest examples of ancient woodland in Britain – can fairly claim to be OF the capital city as it has been owned by the City Corporation for more than a century. The most famous feature of the 540 acre site is the beech pollards, some of which are almost half a millennium old. Given the wood's accessibility (just north of Junction 6 of the M4), it would be the perfect place to get away from it all if it were not for the fact that every year half a million other people have the same idea too! Autumn is the very best time to visit. / Times: *Pedestrians 24 hours, vehicles 08.00- one hour after sunset;* Brit Rail: *Slough (then bus to Farnham Common).*

Bushy Park, Middx
0181-979 1586   off map
This park is part of Wren's grand design for neighbouring Hampton Court Park and boasts a fine chestnut avenue. Herds of red and fallow deer roam its 1100 acres. The Woodland Gardens, with their fine azaleas, camellias and rhododendrons, are a post-war addition. / Times: *Pedestrians, 24 hours; vehicles 6.30-00.00;* Brit Rail: *Hampton Wick.*

Chelsea Harbour SW10
0171-351 4433   3–4B
This contemporary riverside development never seems to have lived up to its aspirations, but it does offer quite an attractive marina, a pleasant place for a riverside walk on a sunny day, and some good views. Given its relatively central location, it has a surprisingly far away feel. / Tube: *Earl's Court (then C3 bus).*

Chiswick House W4
Burlington Lane   0181-995 5390   1–3A
The mainly wooded, 64 acre gardens of this fine neo-classical villa have suitably Italianate highlights – statues, temples, urns and obelisks – and there is also a lake. The information centre (which has a small exhibition about the history of the garden) can equip you with a park trails pamphlet and map. There is a picnic area (and also a café). The house, to which there is an entry charge, is run by the National Trust. / Times: *08.00-dusk;* Tube: *Turnham Green (then E3 bus).*

The mobile phone · For everyday · For everyone

Crane Park Island, Middx

Crane Park, Twickenham   0181-898 9582   off map
This small island (just over 4 acres), reached by bridge, has its place in history – the old gunpowder mill here (now demolished) is believed to have been where Guy Fawkes obtained his supplies. Nowadays, its attractions are rather more peaceful, and it's an agreeable site, run by the London Wildlife Trust. There are three paths, one of which (Hobbin Path) is suitable for disabled people. / Times: *dawn-dusk;* Brit Rail: *Witton.*

Gunnersbury Triangle Nature Reserve W4

Chiswick   1–3A
This six acre site developed a rich covering of vegetation after being surrounded by railway tracks in the late nineteenth century. It has been undisturbed, apart from some allotments, ever since. It was threatened by development in the early 1980s and became a "test case". The conservationists won, and this was the first time that a planning inspector had preferred nature conservation to development on a city site. It is now managed by the London Wildlife Trust. The reserve is open Sunday only at the time of writing – check with the Trust (tel 0171-278 6612) for further information.
/ Tube: *Chiswick Park.*

Hampton Court Palace *, Middx

0181-781 9500   off map
Both the wonderful garden and the park of Wolsey's great riverside palace (completed by Henry VIII and substantially altered by William and Mary) are open to the public without charge. The formal gardens are the most visited free attraction of their type in the country, and include features from Victorian times, as well as from the earlier periods of the palace's construction. Around the gardens, in the 560 acre park, graze the descendants of the deer hunted by the Tudor monarchs. The Great Vine, planted by Capability Brown in 1768, is claimed to be the oldest in the world, and still bears fruit. There is a charge for access to the palace and the maze.
/ Times: *07.00-21.00 (dusk if earlier), 365 days a year;* Brit Rail: *Hampton Court.*

Holland Park W8

Ilchester Place   0171-603 2129   3–1A
Until some 40 years ago, Holland Park was an extraordinary hangover from former days – a private "country" estate, in the middle of London. It maintains a unique and charming character, and, in spite of its relatively small size (54 acres), some of it is heavily wooded (and managed so as to enhance wildlife). It is one of the most attractive parks in London. Apart from its superb formal gardens, it benefits from a recent addition in the form of the Kyoto Garden, installed by Japanese benefactors in 1991. Other attractions include a large play-park and the Ecology Centre, which has a series of free talks and events. The park contains the Orangery and the Ice House (see also). / Times: *07.30-30 mins before dusk;* Tube: *Holland Park, Kensington High Street.*

The mobile phone • For everyday • For everyone

Hyde Park W2

0171-298 2000   3–1C

The greatest of the central Royal Parks was originally acquired by Henry VIII from the Abbey at Westminster as a private hunting ground. Its 340 acres now offer a variety of attractions, ranging from the formal gardens along its south side, to Rotten Row (a bridleway for more than 300 years), a river (the Serpentine) and areas of woods and grass, designed to look like an idealised vision of rural England. In the summer, there are concerts at the bandstand (afternoons and evenings on Sundays and Bank Holidays). Speakers' Corner (see also) is situated in the north east corner of the park. Kensington Gardens (effectively the continuation of Hyde Park to the west) also has its own entry. / Times: 05.00-00.00; Tube: Knightsbridge, Hyde Park Corner, Marble Arch, Lancaster Gate, Queensway.

Kensington Gardens W8

0171-298 2100   3–1B

These were the private gardens of Kensington Palace (which was designed by Wren) and were largely laid out under the direction of Queen Caroline. The gardens were opened to the public by Queen Victoria and are now effectively an extension of Hyde Park. Attractions in the 275 acres include the Boating Pond (model boats only, please), the charming small statue of Peter Pan and the very pretty area in the immediate vicinity of the palace itself. The gardens also house the Serpentine Gallery (see also) and the Highest Free-standing Scaffolding in the World (formerly known as the Albert Memorial). In summer, there are weekly concerts at the bandstand. / Times: Dawn-dusk; Tube: Bayswater, Lancaster Gate, Queensway, High Street Kensington.

Marble Hill House *, Middx

Richmond Road, Twickenham   0181-892 5115   off map

Built in the 1720s as a retreat from court life for Henrietta Howard, Countess of Suffolk (George II's mistress), this Palladian villa – one of the most perfect surviving examples of the type – inhabits a large park which stretches down to the river. The central attraction of the house is the Great Room, with its gilded carving and paintings of Ancient Rome by Panini. A charge is being introduced for admission to the house (but not the gardens) in April 1995. / Times: 10.00-18.00 (Apr-Oct); Wed-Sun 10.00-16.00 (Nov-Mar); Tube: Richmond.

Osterley Park *, Middx

Isleworth   0181-560 3918   off map

This is one of the last great houses with an intact estate in Greater London, set in 140 acres of landscaped park with ornamental lakes. Originally a sixteenth century mansion (built for Sir Thomas Gresham, founder of the Royal Exchange), it was transformed into neo-classical style by Robert Adam in the eighteenth century. It's been a National Trust property for over half a century, but they only took over the management five years ago and are now in the process of restoring the garden to the appearance it would have had two centuries ago. There is a charge for admission to the house and for car parking. / Times: Park: 06.30-19.30 or sunset if earlier; Tube: Osterley.

Portobello Road Market W10, W11
1–2B

On Saturday, Portobello market is undoubtedly the place in West London for combining people-watching and browsing. The street market stretches for over a mile, and in fact comprises several different markets. The most famous, the antiques market, is at the south end, but there is also a food market, bric-à-brac stalls and (under the Westway) a good gathering of vendors of trendy clothing and accessories. / *Tube:* Notting Hill Gate, Ladbroke Grove.

Ranelagh Gardens SW3
Royal Hospital Road   3–3D

Apart from when they are cordoned off every year for the famous Chelsea Flower Show (in May), these well kept gardens lead a rather low-profile life. They are, however, unusually pretty and intimate. A visit here combines very well with one to the neighbouring Royal Hospital (see also). / *Times:* 10.00 (Sun 14.00)–30 mins before dusk, but closed 13.00-14.00; *Tube:* Sloane Square.

Riverside Walks
See the South section for suggestions of interesting walks by the Thames.

Ruislip Woods, Middx
Ruislip   01895 250635   off map

These 700 acres include, in the 250 acre Park Wood, the largest unbroken area of woodland in London. A particular attraction of the Bayhurst Wood Country Park, which forms another part of the woods, is its barbecue sites – although there is a charge to book these, you don't have to pay if you are prepared to take "pot luck" – and there are also picnic sites. "A short guide to Ruislip Woods" is available in local libraries or write to Recreation Unit, Local Services, Civic Centre, Uxbridge, Middx UB8 1UW. / *Brit Rail:* Ruislip (then H13, Sun 114 bus).

Highgate Wood N6
Muswell Hill Road   0181-444 6129   off map
The 70 acres of Highgate Wood were taken over by the Corporation of London as "an open space for ever" in 1886. There's a small playground and a sports ground, but the attraction is essentially what the name suggests – an ancient woodland, with diverse flora and fauna, all just a few yards from the Archway Road. If you're planning to spend more than an hour or so in the wood it would be worth investing in the City's attractively illustrated booklet (small charge), which lists the flora, birds and butterflies which can be spotted there. You might also like to explore the neighbouring 48 acre Queen's Wood (across the Muswell Hill Road), which is relatively wild and boasts an equally impressive selection of wildlife. / Tube: Highgate.

Parkland Walk N22, N8, N4
Haringey   0181-348 6005
Walking down a railway line might seem a rather hazardous activity, but the redundant line between Finsbury Park station and Alexandra Palace offers an interesting option for a country walk in town. The total length of the walk is 4 1/2 miles, and it takes two hours, they say. For a leaflet (which includes a map) contact the Haringey Conservation Officer on the number given. / Tube: Finsbury Park.

Primrose Hill NW3
0171-486 7905   4–3B
The hill – the 61 acre continuation of Regent's Park to the north – is by far the most central natural vantage point over London, and is therefore justly celebrated for its views. In winter, it's an extremely atmospheric place to go tobogganing, and one of the largest bonfire parties in town takes place here every November. / Times: 24 hours; Tube: Chalk Farm/Camden Town.

Queen's Park NW6
Kingswood Avenue   0181-969 5661   1–2B
A 30 acre Kilburn park owned and run by the Corporation of London since 1886. It's not particularly large, but is popular in this relatively under-provided part of town. It's an especially good park for children, with its large, supervised playground, its paddling pool and its "pets village" (including sheep, rabbits, chickens and ducks). There is also an ornamental garden and a fine, Victorian bandstand, recently restored to its original colour scheme. Each September sees a community entertainment day – involving music, comedy and games – which draws big crowds. / Times: 07.00-dusk; Tube: Queen's Park.

Railway Fields N4
(Opp. Haringey/Green Lanes Station)   0181-348 6005   1–1C
This conservation park, in a former British Rail goods yard, has been developed for teaching primary school children about nature. There is a meadow, a woodland and a pond, and even a unique hybrid plant – the Haringey Knotweed. A visitor centre, with leaflets, provides information about the ecology of the site (as well as other places of environmental interest in the borough). / Times: Mon-Fri 10.00-17.00 (phone ahead to confirm); Tube: Manor House.

The mobile phone • For everyday • For everyone

Regent's Canal Towpath

Created as part of Nash's design for Regent's Park, the eight or so miles of canal run from the docks in the east, through Camden at Camden Lock, NW1, along the north of the Park and on to the waterway's conclusion in Paddington (where it meets the Grand Union Canal). There is a tow-path along most of its length and the prettiest part is towards its western conclusion in the extremely attractive stretch through Little Venice, W9. A leaflet "Explore London's Canals", which also covers walks on the Grand Union Canal is available if you send an sae to British Waterways (London Canals), Toll House, Delamere Terrace, Little Venice, London W2 6ND.

Regent's Park NW1

0171-486 7905   4–3B

Regent's Park's 297 acres have an atmosphere all of their own, perhaps because the park was in fact designed as a grand garden suburb. In the end, only eight of the 26 villas which Nash planned at the beginning of the last century were built (though a few more have recently been added). During the summer, music is performed on a regular basis, at the bandstand or at various other points around the park. Queen Mary's Rose Garden has one of the finest selections of blooms in the country and the lake boasts an impressive variety of wildfowl. / Times: 05.00-30 mins before dusk; Tube: Regent's Park, Baker Street, Camden Town, Great Portland Street.

Roundwood Park NW10

Harlesden Road   0181-900 5653   1–2A

A fine 60 acre Victorian park in Willesden (celebrating its centenary in 1995), with impressive floral displays and an aviary stocked with exotic birds. There is also a new children's playground.
/ Times: 08.00-dusk; Tube: Willesden Green.

Waterlow Park N6

Highgate Park   1–1C

Given to the public by Sir Sydney Waterlow in 1889, this "garden for the gardenless" is situated on a steep hillside and has an unusual three-level lake, formal gardens and terraces. Lauderdale House (see also) is within the park. Facilities include a children's play area.
/ Times: 07.30-dusk; Tube: Highgate.

South London

Introduction

South London boasts many of the best free destinations, especially for a family day out.

Just over Chelsea Bridge, Battersea Park is the only one of the central parks to benefit from a river frontage, and offers a wide range of attractions. A little further south, Dulwich Park is very fine, and a visit there can be combined with one to The Horniman Museum, a gem of a place both for its collections and its gardens; (or, on Friday only, a visit to the Dulwich Picture Gallery is also a possibility). Crystal Palace Park is also an interesting destination (especially on Sunday afternoon, when the exhibition about the Palace is open).

To the South East, Greenwich, with Greenwich Park, the Royal Naval College and the Old Royal Observatory, makes an excellent destination for a day out, and the Thames Barrier is not far away. At the weekend, you can also stroll around Greenwich Market. To the south west, Richmond, and the great adjoining Richmond Park is also a very attractive place for a full day's exploration (especially bearing in mind the attractions around Twickenham, just on the other side of the river - see West).

If you're heading back to central London from some of the more grown-up cultural attractions south of the river, such as the Imperial War Museum, it's worth bearing in mind that the early evening sees some of London's best free music at the Royal National Theatre and the Royal Festival Hall

Greenwich Tourist Information Centre SE10
46 Greenwich Church Street   0181-858 6376   1–3D
J / Times: 10.15-16.45 (May-Oct); Mon-Thu 11.00-16.00, Fri-Sun 10.15-16.45 (Nov-Apr); Brit Rail: Greenwich.

Lewisham Tourist Information Centre SE13
199-201 Lewisham High Street   0181-297 8317   1–4D
/ Times: Mon-Fri 09.00 (Mon 10.00)-17.00; Brit Rail: Lewisham.

Richmond Tourist Information Centre, Surrey
The Old Town Hall, Whittacker Avenue, Richmond   0181-940 9125   off map
/ Times: Mon-Fri 10.00-18.00, Sat 10.00-17.00, Sun (May-Oct only) 10.15-16.15; Tube: Richmond.

The mobile phone • For everyday • For everyone

Indoor attractions

Age Exchange Reminiscence Centre SE3
11 Blackheath Village   0181-318 9105   1–4D
*Everyday objects from the past are set out in a charming 1930s
shop. This "hands on museum of the 1930s and 1940s" should
interest both anyone who can remember those days, as well as those
who cannot. There is a changing temporary exhibition at the rear.
The café serves tea and cakes in period style.*
/ *Times: Mon-Fri 10.00-17.30; Brit Rail: Blackheath.*

Avery Hill Winter Garden SE9
Avery Hill Park, Avery Hill Road   081-316 8991   off map
*Bananas grow in south London! There is also a fine collection of cacti
in this imposing domed glasshouse, originally built as a private winter
garden by one Colonel North (who died in 1900). There are cold,
temperate and semi-tropical houses.* / *Times: 10.00-12.00, 13.00-16.00;
Brit Rail: Falconwood.*

Battersea Arts Centre * SW11
Lavender Hill   0171-223 2223   1–4B
*The gallery of this busy arts centre, housed in Battersea's fine former
Town Hall, holds regularly changing exhibitions. There is generally a
charge for the other attractions, but it's certainly worth picking up
one of their monthly calendars to look out for the occasional free
events.* / *Times: Mon 10.00-18.00, Tue-Sat 10.00-22.00, Sun 11.00-22.00;
Tube: South Kensington (then 45A bus).*

Bexley Museum, Kent
Hall Place, Bourne Road, Bexley   01322 526574   off map
*The museum contains permanent displays on local geology, natural
history and archaeology, plus a Victorian bathroom display. There are
varied temporary exhibitions, mostly on a local history theme.*
/ *Times: Mon-Sat 10.00-17.00, Sunday (summer only) 14.00-18.00; Tube: Bexley.*

Black Cultural Museum SW9
378 Coldharbour Lane   0171-738 4591   1–4C
*Every aspect of the history of black people in Britain is covered by
the collections of this Brixton museum. There are also changing
exhibitions and displays of work by black artists.*
/ *Times: Mon-Sat 10.00-18.00; Tube: Brixton.*

Bromley Museum, Kent
The Priory, Church Hill, Orpington   01689-873826   off map
*This local museum covers the history of the neighbourhood from
prehistoric times and includes a mammoth's tusk. Reflecting the
area's great period of expansion, there is some emphasis on the
social history of the 1930s. A display commemorates Sir John
Lubbock, the first Lord Avebury (1834-1913), whom we have to
thank for Bank Holidays. There is a programme of temporary
exhibitions throughout the year.* / *Times: Mon-Wed, Fri &
Sat 09.00-17.00; Brit Rail: Orpington.*

The mobile phone • For everyday • For everyone

Cuming Museum SE17

155-157 Walworth Road, Southwark   0171-701 1342   1–3C
Southwark is one of the most historically interesting parts of London. Its museum (situated just south of the Elephant and Castle) has a rather unusual basis, being derived largely from the objects collected by the Cuming family between 1786 and 1902, and it includes important items such as the dynamo built by Faraday. On a more modern theme, there are usually temporary exhibitions, including interactive displays to keep the kids happy. Occasionally, there are early-evening talks on a wide range of topics. The summer holidays usually see special events for the children. / Times: Tue-Sat 10.00-17.00; Tube: Elephant & Castle.

Dulwich Picture Gallery * SE21

College Road   0181-693 5254;
recorded information 0181-693 8000   1–4C
The first public picture gallery in the UK (1814), designed by Sir John Soane and almost as notable for its neo-classical design as for its very important collection of old masters, which includes works by Rembrandt, Van Dyck, Claude and Poussin. There is a particularly good selection of seventeenth century Dutch art and also some of the greatest portraits by Gainsborough and Reynolds. Perhaps because its scale is not at all intimidating, this is one of the most enjoyable galleries to visit and the building has great atmosphere. A curiosity at its centre is the mausoleum, which contains sarcophagi of the museum's founders. Combine a visit here with one to Dulwich Park (see also), opposite. / Times: Fri 10.00-17.00; Brit Rail: North Dulwich or West Dulwich.

Eltham Palace SE9

Tilt Yard Approach, Court Road   0181-294 2548   off map
Both Henry VIII and Elizabeth I spent much of their childhood here – a place which has belonged to the Crown since 1305. Only the Great Hall, with its impressive hammer-beam roof remains, but it is an interesting site, approached over London's oldest bridge, dating from the fifteenth century. The elevated location affords good views over London. / Times: Thu & Sun 10.00-18.00 (16.00 winter); Brit Rail: Eltham.

Erith Museum, Kent

Erith Library, Walnut Tree Rd, Erith   01322-336582   off map
Situated on the second floor of Erith Library, this small museum features displays of local history, with an Edwardian kitchen and exhibits relating to local industries and the River Thames.
/ Times: Mon, Wed, Sat 14.15-17.15 (Sat 17.00); Brit Rail: Erith.

George Inn SE1

77 Borough High Street   0171-407 2056   5–4C
The only remaining galleried coaching inn in London, seventeenth century in origin, really is a public house (leased by the National Trust to Whitbreads) so anyone can go and have a look at its interior, parts of which are extremely characterful.
/ Times: Mon-Sat 11.00-11.00, Sun 12-3, 19.00-22.30; Tube: London Bridge.

Greenwich Borough Museum SE18

232 Plumstead High Street   0181-855 3240   off map
The permanent displays at this local museum (housed on the upper floor of Plumstead Library) concentrate on local geology, archaeology and wildlife. More recent periods are represented by collections of household and personal items, and there is a programme of temporary exhibitions. Children's activities are organised on Saturdays and during school holidays. | Times: Mon 14.00 – 19.00; Tue & Thu-Sat 10.00 – 13.00 and 14.00 - 17.00; Brit Rail: Plumstead.

Honeywood Heritage Centre, Surrey

Honeywood Walk, Carshalton   0181-773 4555   off map
On the edge of the Carshalton Village ponds, this seventeenth century house contains an exhibition setting out the local history of the borough of Sutton, which includes an audio-visual display. Many of the rooms have been refurbished in period style, including the Billiard Room (in an early twentieth century annex), a 'children's room' which houses a number of Edwardian toys, and the Tudor Gallery. | Times: Thu 10.00-13.00; Brit Rail: Carshalton.

Horniman Museum SE23

London Road   0181-699 1872   1–4D
"Free Museum" is carved in stone at the entrance of this fascinating Forest Hill museum (adjacent to delightful, very well-maintained gardens which boast a bandstand and lovely views over London). A visit here has something for everyone. It grew out of the enthusiasms of Victorian tea magnate Frederick Horniman, who in 1897 opened this art nouveau gallery to house his collection. It is divided into natural history, musical instruments and ethnography, and contains many fascinating, very well-structured exhibits, with the aquarium a particular highlight. There is a good programme of talks and workshops in the museum, and music in the bandstand. | Times: Mon-Sat 10.30-17.30, Sun 14.00-17.30; Brit Rail: Forest Hill.

Imperial War Museum * SE1

Lambeth Road   0171-416 5000;
recorded information 0171-820 1683   2–4D
This fine museum's collection of planes, tanks and every imaginable weapon of war extends to all of the conflicts in which British and Commonwealth forces have been involved since 1914, and it stages some spectacular exhibits, using inter-active video technology. These include the Blitz Experience, complete with sounds and smells. The museum also has a large collection of British art. | Times: 16.30-18.00; Tube: Lambeth North, Elephant & Castle.

Kingston Museum, Surrey

Wheatfield Way   0181-546 5386   off map
This purpose-built Edwardian museum now (after recent renovation) houses two major exhibitions. One, Kingston Families, is a new display of clothing and other mementoes of prominent local families. The other, Ancient Origins, illustrates the borough's past from pre-history to Anglo-Saxon times. It is hoped to open Town of Kings, the continuation of the story to the present day, in 1996. There is also an art gallery in which temporary exhibitions are held. | Times: Mon, Tue, Thu-Sat 10.00-17.00; Brit Rail: Kingston.

The mobile phone • For everyday • For everyone

Livesey Museum SE15

682 Old Kent Road   0171-639 5604   1–3D
Southwark's museum for children presents a lively and varied programme of "hands-on" exhibitions. They are principally directed at the under-12s, but parents and other minders are quite free to take part. / Times: *Mon-Sat 10.00-17.00;* Tube: *Elephant & Castle (then 53 or 172 bus).*

London Glass Blowing Workshop SE1

7 Leather Market, Weston Street   0171-403 2800   5–4C
This well-established glass-blowing business has recently moved into new premises. You are welcome to pay a visit to watch the molten glass being blown and moulded, and if you so wish you can, of course, buy one of their colourful artefacts on the way out. / Times: *Mon-Fri 10.00-17.00;* Tube: *London Bridge, Borough.*

Museum of Artillery in the Rotunda SE18

Repository Road, Woolwich   0181-316 5402   off map
A fine museum, housed in a quite extraordinary Nash building. It began life as a huge replica bell tent, used as a marquee in the grounds of the Prince Regent's home at Carlton House, and was relocated to its present site in 1819. The wide-ranging collection within it illustrates the development of artillery from its very beginnings to the present day (and includes, for example, parts of the Iraqi "supergun"). The policy of free entry and the opening hours are being reviewed in early 1995. / Times: *Mon-Fri 12.00-17.00; Sat-Sun 13.00-17.00 (16.00 Nov-Mar);* Brit Rail: *Woolwich Arsenal.*

Museum of Garden History SE1

Lambeth Palace Road   0171-261 1891   2–4D
A replica seventeenth century garden is part of the attraction of this South Bank museum, attractively housed in a former church. Exhibits explain the history of gardening, and there is a large collection of historic gardening tools and other memorabilia. / Times: *Sun-Fri 10.30-16.00 (Sun 17.00);* Tube: *Waterloo or Victoria (then 507 bus, or C10 on Sun).*

Photofusion SW9

17A Electric Lane   0171-738 5774   1–4C
This Brixton gallery has monthly-changing shows by leading photographers. / Times: *Tue-Fri 10.30-17.30, Sat 12.00-16.00;* Tube: *Brixton.*

Puppet Centre Trust SW11

BAC, Lavender Hill   0171-228 5335   1–4B
Muffin the Mule is – at least for those of more mature years – the undoubted star of the trust's fine collection of puppets, rare photographs, slides, posters and memorabilia. The policy of free admission here is under review. / Times: *Mon-Fri 14.00-18.00;* Tube: *South Kensington (then 45A bus).*

The mobile phone • For everyday • For everyone

The Royal Festival Hall * SE1

0171-928 3002   2–3C

The concert hall at the centre of Europe's largest cultural complex offers a range of "free foyer events", all of which are set out in the centre's colourful monthly programme. There's almost always something on between 12.30 and 14.00 – usually music and often of high quality.

During the summer, there is the "Great Outdoors" series of events on the river terraces and sometimes even on the roof – on one August evening in 1994, for example, you could have enjoyed "a live late night collaboration … featuring a double-screened animated film, body movement and music on the side of the Queen Elizabeth Hall wall". The week-long "Ballroom Blitz", which gives you the opportunity to have a go at almost any type of dancing, is another annual fixture. While you're visiting the centre, you can take in one of the ever-changing exhibitions in the Festival Hall Galleries, which are open all day and evening.

If you visit the Hall towards the end of the day, the view across the Thames from the upper terrace is one of the finest in London. To conclude a visit here, you might consider taking in the foyer music at 18.00 at the nearby Royal National Theatre (see also).
/ *Times:* 10.00-22.30; *Tube:* Embankment, Waterloo.

The Royal National Theatre * SE1

South Bank   0171-633 0880   2–3D

Its uncompromising exterior may have taken a while to win Londoners' affections, but the interior of Sir Denys Lasdun's riverside building has always found favour with theatre-goers. Even if you're not going to a show, you can still explore the various levels of the intriguing layout and you can also have a look around one or more of the several concurrent exhibitions, which are open all day every day (except Sunday). Or take in the music – it might be early or contemporary, classical, folk or jazz – at 18.00 nightly and 13.00 on Saturdays. / *Times:* Mon-Sat 10.00-23.00; *Tube:* Embankment, Waterloo.

Royal Naval College SE10

King William Walk, Greenwich   0181-858 2154   1–3D

Wren's baroque Greenwich Hospital (for retired sailors) became the Royal Naval College in 1873. The extraordinary Painted Hall (whose entire interior is decorated with paintings by James Thornhill) should not be missed, and the attractive eighteenth century chapel (decorated by Athenian Stuart) is also worth a visit.
/ *Times:* Fri-Wed 14.30-16.30; *Brit Rail:* Greenwich.

South London Art Gallery SE15

65 Peckham Road   0171-703 6120   1–3C

This elegant Victorian gallery was re-opened in 1993. It shares its site with the well-known Camberwell College of Arts. The gallery presents a changing programme of innovative contemporary works by international artists. / *Times:* Tue, Wed & Fri 11.00-18.00, Thu 11.00-19.00, Sat & Sun 14.00-18.00; *Brit Rail:* Peckham Rye.

Southwark Cathedral SE1
Montague Close   0171-407 2939   5–4C
Thirteenth century in origin (but with many later alterations), this fine building, just over London Bridge, is something of a hidden gem. Being rather overshadowed by the fame of the cathedrals on the other side of the river, it benefits from an absence of crowds. It is, in fact, the oldest Gothic church in London (and was apparently the inspiration for the design of Westminster Abbey). Nor does it want for historical associations – the Bard's brother, Edward Shakespeare was buried here in 1607, and that same year saw the baptism of John Harvard, founder of the University. There is an organ recital on Monday lunchtime and a music recital on Tuesday.
/ *Times: 08.30-18.00; Tube: London Bridge.*

Wimbledon Society's Museum SW19
Village Club, Ridgeway, 26 Lingfield Road   off map
This small, voluntarily run museum depicts the history of Wimbledon from prehistory to the present day. Until recently, of course, Wimbledon was at a good remove from the metropolis, and its rural past is well illustrated by the collection of watercolours, photographs and prints. To find the museum, leave the Common at the corner of Southside and the Green, and go down Lingfield Road.
/ *Times: Sat 14.30-17.00; Tube: Wimbledon.*

Woodlands Art Gallery SE3
90 Mycenae Road   0181-858 5847   off map
This Georgian house has a great artistic tradition. It was built for John Julius Angerstein (the "father of the Lloyds insurance market"), whose extraordinary accumulation of paintings was, after his death, acquired by the government to form the basis of the National Gallery's collection. Woodlands now presents exhibitions of contemporary art changing every month (often by well-known artists) and media exhibited include sculpture, ceramics and photographs. The building, situated in a pretty garden, is shared with the local history library (closed Wed and Fri; tel 0181-858 4631), through whose exhibits visitors are welcome to browse. / *Times: Mon, Tue & Thu-Sat 11.00-17.00, Sun 14.00-17.00; Brit Rail: Westcombe Park.*

Outdoor attractions

Battersea Park SW11
Albert Bridge Road   0181-871 7530   3–4D
This 200 acre park is one of the most popular, most central family destinations and rightly so as it's full of things to look at and do. The long river frontage (punctuated by the Peace Pagoda given to the people of London in 1985 by a Japanese Buddhist Order) has lovely views across the river to Chelsea and the Royal Hospital. Other attractions include the Pump House art gallery, a herb garden, a deer enclosure and London's largest adventure playground for 5 to 16 year olds. There is some excellent literature available from the Park Office (to the left of the Albert Bridge entrance), including "Introducing Battersea Park", which has a map, and really well produced tree and nature trail brochures. / Times: 08.00-dusk; Tube: Sloane Square (then 19 or 137 bus).*

Bermondsey Antiques Market SE1
Bermondsey Square   1–3C
If you arrive at dawn, you'll have missed the best bargains at London's largest antiques markets. As the sun rises, the professionals depart, and the trippers take over. / Times: Fri 05.00 (or earlier)-13.00; Tube: Borough, Elephant & Castle.

Blackheath SE3
0181-305 1807   1–3D
There is not much one can say about this large, flat expanse of grass, which separates the pretty village of Blackheath from Greenwich Park. A couple of pools (one of them a boating pond), aside, its attraction is as a big, open space for running about on and it is an ideal venue for London's annual Kite Festival – see also. / Brit Rail: Blackheath.

Brixton Market SW9
Brixton Station Road   1–4C
The warren of streets and alleys around Brixton tube station houses as exotic a market as you will find in London, with food and fabrics from all around the globe, as well as heaps of the more mundane items you would expect to find anywhere. / Times: Mon-Sat 08.00-17.30 (Wed 13.00); Tube: Brixton.

Crystal Palace Park SE19
Sydenham   0181-778 7148   off map
The Crystal Palace – an enormous glasshouse designed by Sir Joseph Paxton – was originally erected in Hyde Park in 1851. After it had served as the exhibition hall of the Great Exhibition, it was dismantled and moved to Sydenham, where it survived until being consumed by fire in 1936. There's a small museum about the fascinating history of the Palace (tel 0181-676 0700), open 11.00-17.00 on Sundays only, but you can always explore the site. The palace-site is only part of this large and attractive park, which also contains amongst its free attractions a maze and a children's play area. There is also a unique collection of Victorian full-scale models of dinosaurs. / Times: 07.00-dusk; Tube: Crystal Palace.

Dulwich Park SE21

College Road   0171-525 1554   1–4C

A fine collection of trees is the particular attraction of this fine 75 acre Victorian park. The rhododendrons and azaleas are a feature, and for these May is the time to visit. There is a regular programme of guided walks and group events, organised by the Park Ranger service throughout the year. The neighbouring Bel Air Park, of 30 acres, was laid out in the late eighteenth century, in the classic English landscape style – it is relatively little known, but well worth having a look at. A visit to this area on a Friday can be combined with one to the Dulwich Picture Gallery or the Horniman Museum (see also). / Times: *08.00-dusk;* Brit Rail: *North Dulwich or West Dulwich.*

Green Chain Walk

The Green Chain Walks are a twisting network of over 15 miles of well-signposted routes. They link many of South East London's fine parks and open spaces into walks which contain as much greenery as possible. Leaflets detailing the walks (Thamesmead or Erith to Oxleas Wood; Thames Barrier to Oxleas Wood; Oxleas Wood to Mottingham; and Mottingham to Crystal Palace or Chislehurst Common) are available from South East London Libraries.

Greenwich Foot Tunnel SE10

1–3D

The tunnel, opened in 1902, connects Greenwich with the Isle of Dogs and was built because the steamboat ferry was contributing to excessive congestion of the river at this point. Just under a quarter of a mile long, it lies 10 metres below the low water mark and is made of cast iron segments, lined with concrete and tiled. New lifts were installed in 1992, replacing equipment which had lasted since 1904; the original wood panelling was maintained, however. Although the tunnel has a mainly practical function, children of all ages may feel that walking under the Thames is an end in itself. / Times: *Lift service – Mon-Sat 08.30-19.00, Sun 10.00-17.30;* Brit Rail: *Greenwich, Island Gardens (DLR).*

Greenwich Markets SE10

1–3D

If you enjoy nosing around market stalls, it's well worth making a special weekend journey to Greenwich, which has what is possibly the most comprehensive – as well as the most attractively situated – series of market-places in London. The individual markets are: Bosun's Yard (crafts), Greenwich Church Street; the Antiques Market, Greenwich High Road; the Central Market (general), Stockwell Street; the Craft Market, Greenwich Church Street; and, on Sunday only, the Flea Market, Thames Street. / Times: *Sat & Sun 09.00-17.00 (most markets);* Brit Rail: *Greenwich.*

The mobile phone • For everyday • For everyone

South London

Greenwich Park SE10

0181-858 2608   1–3D

This is the oldest of London's Royal Parks (enclosed in 1433) and one of the best destinations offering something for all the family. There has been a deer park here since the fifteenth century, and there are, of course, flower gardens and a children's playground. The unique attraction is the view from the top of the hill by the Old Royal Observatory (see also). In summer, there are Sunday afternoon and evening concerts and there is a family day in July. Don't miss the new Information Centre (at the St Mary's Gate entrance) which has rooms explaining the history and wildlife of the park.
/ *Times:* Dawn-dusk; *Brit Rail:* Greenwich.

Ham House, Surrey *

Ham, Richmond   0181-940 1950   off map

There is a charge for admission to this outstanding Stuart house, which has recently been restored and reopened by the National Trust. Admission to the interesting garden – 17th century in origin and currently in the process of restoration – is, however, free of charge, and you can picnic in the Rose Garden. / *Times:* Sat-Thu 10.30-18.00 (dusk, if earlier); *Tube:* Richmond (then 65 or 371 bus).

Lesnes Abbey Woods, Kent

Lesnes Abbey Road, Belvedere   0181-312 9717   off map

Taking its name from the twelfth century abbey whose remains still stand, this 200 acre wood, together with the adjoining Bostall Heath and woods (160 acres), makes up one of the largest areas of trees in south London. The spring sees a tremendous show of wild daffodils, and then wood anenomes and bluebells. A rather unusual attraction is the fossil bed, in which the public can search for pre-historic remains. The woods are quite hilly and it's a good idea to take some stout footwear. / *Tube:* Abbey Wood.

Morden Hall Park, Surrey

Morden Hall Road, Morden   0181-648 1845   off map

This informal 125 acre park, owned by the National Trust, was laid out around 1860 as a deer park. It is given additional interest by a complex network of waterways coming off the river Wandle (which were designed to be partly ornamental and partly to power snuff mills, whose buildings still stand). You can also visit the craft workshops, and watch local artists and artisans at work.
/ *Times:* Dawn-dusk; *Tube:* Morden.

Old Royal Observatory * SE10
Greenwich Park   1–3D

You can bestride two hemispheres at the top of the hill in Greenwich Park. There's a charge to go inside the charming seventeenth century Observatory (which has one of London's few surviving Wren interiors), but the "0 degree" line is marked outside as well. Many people consider that a photograph with one foot on either side of the Greenwich Mean line is an obligatory souvenir.

The Observatory is the spiritual home of the "Greenwich Time Signal". A longer-established visual sign of time passing is the red ball on top of the Observatory, which descends its pole at exactly 13.00 every day – the original purpose of this signal was to enable seafarers to set their chronometers correctly.

The view from outside the Observatory is possibly the best in London and also summarises the history of London. Immediately ahead, you see the city's imperial past (the Royal Naval College), to the West is the sprawling mass of the City and central London, and, across the river, looms what is perhaps the future – the great mass of Canary Wharf. / Times: Dawn to dusk; Brit Rail: Greenwich.

Oxleas Woods SE10
One of the capital's last remaining ancient woodlands (some 8,000 years old) and only recently saved from the road-builder's bulldozer. The wood supports over 33 different species of tree and shrub, including the rare wild service tree, the hornbeam and guelder rose. Fungi proliferate, with more than 200 species, including the "storybook" toadstool (red with white spots) the poisonous fly agaric. The wood forms part of the Green Chain Walk (see also). There is parking within the woods, accessible from Shooters Hill (A207) and some of the other surrounding roads. / Brit Rail: Falconwood.

Richmond Park, Surrey
0181-948 3209   1–4A

This enormous park (2,385 acres) was created by Charles I by enclosing farmlands. It has changed little in the last 300 years, and still contains some 700 red and fallow deer. Because it has been little disturbed, it offers some rare natural habitats and has been declared a Site of Special Scientific Interest. The Isabella Plantation (towards the Kingston Gate) is noted for its fabulous collection of azaleas, and views from King Henry's Mound stretch as far as the City.
/ Times: Pedestrians, 24 hours; traffic, dawn–30 mins before dusk; Tube: Richmond.

The mobile phone • For everyday • For everyone

Riverside Walks

Arguably the finest walking in London, and certainly some of its best vistas, can be enjoyed on the mostly continuous paths which runs along the Thames, on both the north and south banks from Kingston in the west to Docklands in the east.

The south bank is on balance the better place to walk, because the path is less interrupted and generally more peaceful (and also because, almost invariably, the north bank is the more picturesque to look over to). If you get bored, it is rarely too long before a bridge allows you to swap sides.

The most rural-feeling of the more central stretches of the river is the (often muddy) towpath on the south bank between Putney Bridge and Barnes Bridge. A good walk is to pick up the towpath at the half-way point at Hammersmith Bridge and to walk down to Barnes Bridge, circling back on the north bank, which is also pretty in this area. (It is also worth bearing in mind the numerous pubs at Hammersmith.)

In the centre of town, there is a continuous fine stretch of river between the Houses of Parliament and Tower Bridge, with a magnificent vista of St Pauls when walking east into the City. On the north bank's Victoria Embankment, and later the path in the City, the walk is absolutely continuous and ends up at the picturesque Tower of London and St Katherine's Dock (see also).

One of the nicest places for a gentle stroll on the same stretch of river is away from the traffic, on the south bank between the South Bank Centre and Westminster Bridge. It enjoys similarly magnificent views (especially, when walking west, of the Houses of Parliament) and is a particularly nice walk at night. One of the best views in London is to be had from the footbridge built into Hungerford railway bridge (between Embankment Tube and the South Bank Centre).

Other walks worth bearing in mind are the riverside path in Battersea Park, the north bank to the east of Kew bridge, and, further out of town, the extremely pretty stretch at Richmond.

Surrey Docks Farm SE16

Rotherhithe Street   0171-231 1010   1–3D
This well equipped city farm is in a slightly "away from it all", picturesque location, on the banks of the Thames opposite Canary Wharf. As well as animals – goats, sheep, cows, pigs, chickens, geese, ducks and a donkey – they count amongst their attractions an orchard, a blacksmith's forge, a herb garden, beehives and a bee-room (and it is possible in autumn for kids to help collect the honey). Family visits are free but there is a charge for groups. / Times: Tue-Sun 10.00-17.00 (closed Fri in school hols and closed for lunch, from 13.00-14.00, at weekends and during school hols; Brit Rail: Surrey Quays (then P11 bus).

Thames Barrier * SE18
I Unity Way   0181-854 1373   off map
The Thames Barrier is the largest movable anti-flooding protection device in the world – it was built in response to the ever-greater threat posed to low-lying central London by high tides (which have been rising at the rate of about 75 cm a century). It spans the 520 metre Woolwich reach and consists of 10 separate, massive, movable steel gates. The most spectacular time to visit is during the annual test (in September or October), when the entire barrier is raised to block the high tide, but it's an impressive sight at any time. There is a charge for the visitors centre, but not for access to the riverside walk or the children's play-area. / Brit Rail: Charlton.

Vauxhall City Farm SE11
24 St Oswald's Place   0171-582 4204   1–3C
It may be less than an acre in size, but this tiny farm, run on a semi-voluntary basis, can – thanks to the grazing nearby – boast a full range of farm animals, large and small. / Times: Tue-Thu, Sat & Sun 10.30-17.00; Tube: Vauxhall.

Wimbledon Common SW19
0181-788 7655   1–4B
The common extends to nearly two square miles, some of which is quite rough countryside and there are several ponds with much bird-life. It is the setting for one of London's few remaining windmills, which now houses a museum about the history of windmills (including working models) – for which there is a charge, albeit a small one. / Times: 24 hours; Tube: Southfields.

The City

Introduction

The tiny, but very wealthy "Square Mile" is often likened to
a city-state. It has its own ways of doing things which have
been arrived at over practically a millennium of running its
own affairs, and its long history has left it rich in historic
buildings and institutions. Its wealth and importance are
symbolised by its medieval Guildhall, where great state
banquets are often held, and by the great cathedral of St
Paul's. Its other great sights include the Tower of London,
Tower Bridge and The Monument.

Trading and, later, banking were the foundations of the
City's wealth. Today more international banks gather
together here than anywhere else. Sadly, most trading and
banking business nowadays happens over the telephone –
the Stock Exchange, as a trading place, is no more. For the
casual visitor, the only market which can be visited is the
London Metal Exchange, with the Bank of England Museum
providing the only other insight into these sadly now rather
closed worlds. If you want to see institutions at work, the
barristers' Inns of Court are some of the most interesting,
picturesque and immutable of all – yet they are all open to
the public to a greater or lesser extent.

The City is rich with diverse indoor attractions – the Story
of Telecommunications, the National Postal Museum, and,
on its fringes, the Mount Pleasant Sorting Office and the
London Silver Vaults – all of which should be of interest to
older children and adults.

If planning a visit, it's a good idea to arrive in the late
morning and begin by visiting the City Information Office –
there is usually at least one free lunchtime concert in one of
the City's fine churches (many by Wren). Having spent an
afternoon exploring, you can end the day with some early
evening music at the Barbican.

City of London Information Centre EC4
St Paul's Churchyard   0171-332 1456   5–2B
*The City has a conveniently positioned general tourist information
centre right by St Paul's. It has copies of "City Events", an excellent
guide to the musical and other events happening in the City during
that month. It is also the place where tickets for open-days at the
various City Livery companies are available.* / Times: *Mon-Fri 09.30-17.00,
Sat 09.30-12.00;* Tube: *St Paul's.*

Liverpool Street Station Information Centre EC2
5–2D
The office is in the approach to the Underground station.
/ Times: *Mon-Sat 08.15-18.00 (Mon 19.00), Sun 08.30-16.45;*
Tube: *Liverpool Street.*

Indoor attractions

Bank of England Museum EC2
Bartholomew Lane   0171-601 5545   5–2C
Housed within the forbidding building of the Bank itself, the museum is at the very centre of the City of London and traces the history of the Bank from its royal foundation in 1694 right up to the present, with interactive videos bringing its current activities to life. Curiosities include documents relating to George Washington (a former customer), Kenneth Grahame (a former Secretary of the Bank, as well as being the author of The Wind in the Willows) and the original cartoon by James Gillray which satirised the Bank as the "Old Lady of Threadneedle Street". The neo-classical Bank Stock Office by Sir John Soane, recreated for the museum, makes a graceful centrepiece and is used for temporary exhibitions. / Times: Mon-Fri 10.00-17.00; Sun and Bank Hols 11.00-17.00 (summer only); Tube: Bank.

Barbican * EC2
Silk Street   0171-638 4141   5–1B
Love it or hate it, the City's sprawling, concrete arts and residential complex is certainly impressive with its vast concert hall, theatre, cinema and sweeping internal spaces – the biggest arts centre under a single roof anywhere in the world. There is free music in the foyer most days from 17.30 to 18.50 (and also most Sunday lunchtimes) – see the Centre's programme for details – and there are often special theme events on Bank Holiday weekends. / Times: 09.00 (Sun 12.00)-23.00; Tube: Barbican, Moorgate.

Chartered Insurance Institute EC2
20 Aldermanbury   0171-606 3835   5–2C
The Institute's very characterful building (near the Guildhall) houses displays illustrating the history of insurance through the ages, including the world's largest collection of fire-marks – the signs which, in earlier times, indicated that a building was insured, and by whom. It's a good idea to phone first (extension 3274). / Times: Mon-Fri 09.00-17.00; Tube: St Paul's.

Clockmakers' Company Collection EC2
Guildhall Library, Aldermanbury   0171-332 1868   5–2C
The Clockmakers' Company may go back only to 1631, but its collection of clocks goes back to the fourteenth century, and this single-room museum contains a glittering and fascinating selection of time-pieces. There are also some curiosities, such as the first electric clock and one powered by gas. To hear the collection at its best, make sure you are there at noon. / Times: Mon-Fri 09.30-16.45; Tube: St Paul's.

College of Arms EC4

Queen Victoria Street   0171-248 2762   5–3B

The College, which traces its origins to the thirteenth century, is the body empowered by the sovereign to determine everything relating to the granting of new coats of arms, and the right to bear arms which have been granted in the past. The main part of its building is seventeenth century, and there are some impressive wrought iron gates, which are probably a little later in date. The fine Court Room is open for visits and this is one of the finest, secular, period buildings in the City to which the public has access. / Times: *Mon-Fri 10.00-16.00;* Tube: *Blackfriars.*

Guildhall EC1

Gresham Street   0171-332 1460   5–2C

The hall on this site has been the most important secular building in the City since the eleventh century – many important and glittering state banquets take place here. Much of the present building (which is on a spectacular scale) dates from 1440 and, although fire and bomb damage has taken its toll, a fair amount of the original remains. Casual visitors may see only the hall, but pre-booked parties of 10-50 people may also visit the Old Library and the impressive Undercroft. Bookings are dealt with by the Keeper's office, on the number given. / Times: *10.00-17.00 (closed Sun, Oct-Apr);* Tube: *St Paul's.*

Guildhall Library EC2

Aldermanbury   0171-332 1868   5–2C

This elegant library specialises in the history of London. If this is an area which interests you, this is a delightful place to while away a couple of hours, perusing the shelves. / Times: *Mon-Sat 9.30-17.00 (restricted service Sat);* Tube: *Moorgate, Bank, St Paul's.*

LIFFE EC4

Cannon Bridge   0171-379 2628   5–3C

LIFFE – the London International Financial Futures Exchange - is one of the most colourful markets in London. It still operates on the concept of "open outcry", ie shout as loud as you can. Unfortunately, it's not open to the casual visitor, but it is open to parties aged 16+, strictly by prior arrangement. / Tube: *Mansion House, Cannon Street.*

Livery Halls

The proud and ancient livery companies of the City boast a large number of halls some of which are extremely grand and historic. Access to most of them is difficult, but it is worth applying to the City Information Office early in the year for part of the small allocation of tickets which they receive in February of each year. The companies participating in the scheme vary, but have recently included the Goldsmiths, the Tallow Chandlers, the Skinners, the Fishmongers, the Ironmongers and the Haberdashers. It is possible to arrange an appointment to be shown around the magnificent Fishmongers' Hall at other times by contacting their archivist on 0171-626 3531.

The mobile phone • For everyday • For everyone

London Metal Exchange EC3

56 Leadenhall Street   071 264 5555   5–2D

If you actually want a feel of the City at work, there are very few of its financial and commodity markets which both have a physical marketplace (the Stock Exchange, for example, is now a "telephone market"), and also grant access to the general public. This is one of the two (the other being the International Petroleum Exchange – see the East End). If you want to visit, you must, however, call ahead.
/ *Times: Mon-Fri 12.00-13.30; Tube: Monument.*

London Silver Vaults WC2

Chancery House, Chancery Lane   0171-242 3844   2–2D

This intriguing, subterranean shopping mall, with its 38 silver dealers, claims to offer the largest collection of silverware under one roof in the world. All the items are for sale, with prices ranging from £5 to £100,000, but you're quite welcome just to go and browse and (for groups, and by prior arrangement) they will also arrange a talk.
/ *Times: Mon-Fri 09.00-17.20, Sat 09.00-12.50; Tube: Chancery Lane.*

Museum of the Order of St John EC1

St John's Gate, St John's Lane   0171-253 6644   5–1A

The museum contains the most comprehensive collection of items relating to the Order of St John outside Malta, some dating back to the fifteenth century. The St John Ambulance Museum, nearby, traces more than a century's history of first aid in peace and war. Both museums are housed in the intriguing, very romantic-looking sixteenth century building which was originally the entrance to the Priory of Clerkenwell. Tours are given (Tue, Fri, Sat at 11.00 and 14.30), which also take in the Grand Priory Church, with its beautiful twelfth century crypt. / *Times: Mon-Fri 10.00-17.00, Sat 10.00-4.00; Tube: Farringdon, Barbican.*

National Postal Museum EC1

King Edward Street   0171-239 5420   5–2B

The only complete sheet of Penny Blacks – in fact the proof sheet, printed before the main run – is the star attraction of this huge philatelic collection, which, post-1900, is almost completely comprehensive on a world-wide basis. Temporary exhibitions include postal memorabilia other than stamps, and illustrate the 350 year history of the Royal Mail. / *Times: Mon-Fri 09.30-16.30; Tube: St Paul's.*

Old Bailey EC4

Newgate Street   0171-248 3277   5–2B

The Central Criminal Court, as it is more properly called, is the site of London's most notorious trials. All human life is there, and there's usually something intriguing, amusing or just plain bizarre to listen to. If you're only paying a brief visit, the most interesting thing to do is to catch the cross-examination of a witness by a bewigged barrister from the opposing side. / *Times: Mon-Fri 10.30-13.00, 14.00-16.00; Tube: St Paul's, Blackfriars.*

The mobile phone • For everyday • For everyone

Prince Henry's Room EC4
17 Fleet Street   0171-936 2710   5–2A

In one of the few buildings in the City to survive the Great Fire (1666), this single, small room retains its original panelling and plaster work. The naming of the building is honorific only (referring to the eldest son of James I) and it now houses a selection of memorabilia of diarist Samuel Pepys. The curators are enthusiasts for the great man, and will be pleased to share their knowledge with you. / Times: 11.00-14.00 (closed Sun, Bank Hols and Sats before); Tube: Temple.

Royal Mail Mount Pleasant Sorting Office EC1
Farringdon Road   0171-239 2191   5–1A

If you've always wondered how the mail gets distributed, a visit here should answer all your questions. There are tours (lasting over two hours) five times a day (between 10.00 and 18.00, Mon-Fri), which cover the sorting office, the mechanical sorting equipment and the "Mail Rail" – the unique, unmanned underground railway which distributes post around the capital. If you wish to arrange a visit, call the number given to book in. You will have to confirm in writing by two weeks before. Children under 9 are not admitted.
/ Tube: Farringdon, King's Cross.

The Story of Telecommunications EC4
145 Queen Victoria Street   0171-248 7444   5–3B

The only museum in the UK dedicated to telecommunications houses examples of almost every type of phone that has ever been used in this country. This is no static, hands-off display – many of the exhibits bleep, buzz or ring. This is a great show for the children, but probably also quite a nostalgic one for people of any age. Things change so quickly in this world that the equipment you can recall dates you pretty accurately – do you remember the Trimphone, or buttons "A" and "B"? Think carefully before you answer.
/ Times: Mon-Fri 10.00-17.00 (and Sat of Lord Mayor's Show); Tube: St Paul's.

Wesley's Chapel EC1
49 City Road   0171-253 2262   5–1C

John Wesley, the father of Methodism, had his New Chapel and house built in 1778 to the designs of George Dance the Younger. You can visit the chapel, and also Wesley's tomb, which are part of this fine group of Georgian buildings on the northern fringe of the City. (Wesley's House and a museum can also be visited, but for these there is a charge.) / Times: Mon-Sat 10.00-16.00; Tube: Old Street, Moorgate.

The mobile phone • For everyday • For everyone

Outdoor attractions

Broadgate * EC2
0171-588 6565   5–2D
One summer lunchtime, when the weather is hot, why not take in the City's Broadgate development. Most weekdays from 12.30 to 14.00, this Manhattan-style complex of offices, shops and restaurants puts on musical or other entertainments (usually at some point including a display of Spanish dressage with Andalucian horses). Giant chess and draughts sets are provided too. There's a monthly diary of events – Broadgate Live – which you can obtain from the Arena office (or you can call to be put on the mailing list).
/ *Tube: Liverpool Street.*

Inns of Court
5–2A
Lawyers have clustered around the City since the earliest times. Even today, every barrister practising in England and Wales must be a member of one of the four "inns of court" (the Middle and Inner Temples, Gray's Inn and Lincoln's Inn). These bodies are effectively medieval colleges, with their own dining halls, libraries, gardens and chapels. They are also landlords to the barristers' "chambers" (or offices).

All of the inns give the public access to some part of their territories, which are peaceful, charming and often of considerable antiquity.

Starting in the Temple, don't miss Middle Temple Hall, a large Tudor hall with a magnificent hammer-beam roof. This area is also rich in historical trivia: not only was "Twelfth Night" first performed in the hall here by the Bard's own company, but the Wars of the Roses took their name from red and white flowers plucked from the garden behind.

The hall at the neighbouring Inner Temple is not open to the public, but the main sight there is the Temple Church, the only circular church in London and one of London's oldest buildings (twelfth century).

Leaving the Temple, and progressing up Chancery Lane, you come first to Lincoln's Inn, with its fine, sweeping lawns, halls (one fifteenth century, one nineteenth) and library, and then to Gray's Inn, whose medieval (if mainly rebuilt after the war) hall and chapel are open to public view.

The grounds of all the inns are open on weekdays. Mid-morning and mid-afternoons of weekdays are generally the best times to gain access to the halls and chapels – if you are making a special trip, it may be wise to confirm access with the following numbers for the respective inns (all 0171-): Middle Temple (353 4355), Lincoln's Inn (405 1393) and Gray's Inn (405 8164). / Tube: Temple, Chancery Lane.

The Monument * EC2

5–3C

The Great Fire of 1666 swept away much of the medieval City. The burghers of the day commissioned Wren to memorialise this devastation and the Monument - still the highest free-standing stone column in the world — was the result. Its height (202 ft) is the same as its distance from the baker's shop in Pudding Lane where the fire started — the story is given in more detail by the large notice at the column's base. You can climb up to the top, but there's a small charge. / *Tube:* Monument.

Riverside Walks

See the South section for suggestions of interesting walks by the Thames.

Tower Bridge * EC3

0171-407 0922   5–4D

One of London's great symbols, the bridge was built between 1886 and 1894. Despite its appearance, it is, in fact, a thoroughly modern steel structure, but was clad in stone to harmonise with the Tower of London. The two halves of the bridge (which was originally steam-powered, but is now electrically operated) can still be raised to accommodate the occasional large vessel needing access to the Pool of London — ring the number given to find out when the bridge is next scheduled to be raised. There is a fascinating display inside the bridge, but at quite a significant charge. / *Tube:* Tower Hill.

Tower of London * EC3

West Gate, Tower of London   0171-709 0765   5–3D

The Tower of London is one of the most interesting and historic sites in London and unfortunately charges handsomely for entering its precincts or visiting the treasures within (which, of course, include the Crown Jewels). You can get a good perspective of the medieval building from the riverside walk, however (and see also Ceremony of the Keys). / *Tube:* Tower Hill.

The East End

Introduction

Centuries of being the poor relation among the areas of London, has left the East End with a very different range of amenities from any other area. It means for example that in the inner city there is only one park of any note, Victoria Park. However, if you are prepared to go as far as the end of the Central Line, you will, in Epping Forest, find the largest medieval woodland anywhere near London. A feature of the East End (and much less common elsewhere), which is of particular interest to children, is the city farms.

As regeneration of the East End proper takes hold, however, some very notable attractions are springing up. Canary Wharf, the largest office development in Europe, has given the Isle of Dogs the second tallest building in Europe. The redevelopment of St Katharine's Dock has created what is by far the nicest marina in inner London, and, on a sunny day, a really charming place. The continuing efforts to improve the Lee Valley are beginning to make it an amenity which offers a large range of attractions. The area is well served with non-commercial art galleries (the Whitechapel Gallery being the grandest and longest established).

For people-watching and browsing, the area has two of the most characterful markets in London, both particularly popular as Sunday morning destinations – Petticoat Lane and Brick Lane.

London Docklands Visitor Centre E14
3 Limeharbour, Isle of Dogs   0171-512 1111   1–3D
Not just an information centre on what to do in Docklands and East London. There's also an exhibition and a 13 minute audio-visual presentation in the theatre. While you're in the visitor centre, pick up a copy of "London Docklands and East London what to see and do," an attractively presented guide to the local attractions. There's also a good "Street Guide," which includes a usefully indexed map, and a "What's On" guide. / Times: Mon-Fri 09.00-18.00; Sat & Sun 09.30-17.00; Tube: Crossharbour (DLR).

Redbridge Tourist Information Centre
Town Hall, 128-142 High Road, Ilford IG1 1DD
0181-478 3020   off map
/ Times: Mon-Fri 08.30-17.00; Brit Rail: Ilford.

Tower Hamlets Tourist Information Centre E1
107A Commercial Street   0171-375 2549   5–2D
*The Centre is located within Spitalfields Market.
/ Times: Mon-Fri 09.30-16.30; Tube: Liverpool Street.*

Indoor attractions

Bethnal Green Museum of Childhood E2
Cambridge Heath Road   0181-980 3204   1–2D
Housing the V&A's collection of toys, games, puppets, dolls and dolls houses (of which there are over 40), this repository of children's memorabilia offers quite enough to interest children and parents. There are workshops for children most Saturdays, and school holiday activities. / Times: Mon-Thu 10.00-17.50, Sat 10.00-18.00, Sun 14.30-18.00; Tube: Bethnal Green.

Camerawork E2
121 Roman Road   0181-980 6256   1–2D
Exhibitions at this contemporary photographic gallery are usually thematic (often based on social issues) and frequently include less conventional media such as computer output and video. / Times: Tue-Sat 13.00-18.00; Tube: Bethnal Green.

Chisenhale Gallery E3
64 Chisenhale Road   0181-981 4518   1–2D
This contemporary gallery holds half a dozen shows a year by British and foreign artists. There is an emphasis on sculpture and installations. / Times: Wed-Sun 13.00-18.00; Tube: Mile End, Bethnal Green.

Geffrye Museum E2
Kingsland Road   0171-739 9893   1–2C
A rather special museum, located in elegant early eighteenth century almshouses, and telling the story of English domestic interiors through a series of period rooms, from Elizabethan times to the 1950s. There's even an enchanting walled herb garden. In summer they organise unusual, intelligent activities for kids and, in the summer, there is often music (not always period), in either the museum or the garden – ask for a programme. Most Londoners will never have been here – they should go. / Times: Tue-Sat 10.00-17.00, Sun and Bank hols 14.00-17.00; Tube: Liverpool Street, Old Street.

Hackney Museum E8
Central Hall, Mare Street   0181-986 6914   1–1D
The museum celebrates the history of Hackney from Viking times, but it's perhaps the exhibitions reflecting the area's cultural diversity which are the particular attraction. There is a series of workshops for children throughout the year. / Times: Tue-Fri 10.00-12.30 & 13.30-17.00; Sat 13.30-17.00; Tube: Bethnal Green (then 106, 253 or D6 bus).

International Petroleum Exchange E1
International Hs, 1 St Katharine's Way   0171-481 0643   5–3D
One of the few City-related financial markets which you can actually see at work (the other being the London Metal Exchange – see The City). The market operates on the principle of "open outcry", and the best time to visit is in the early afternoon. Members of the public are welcome to arrange visits (which must be pre-booked), but should try to give a reasonable amount of notice. / Tube: Tower Hill.

The mobile phone • For everyday • For everyone

London Gas Museum E3

Twelvetrees Crescent   0171-987 2000x3344   1–2D
A small museum, illustrating the history of the gas industry (and what life was like before gas). There is an exhibit commemorating the Beckton Gasworks (in nearby E16) which were, in their time, the largest in the world. / Times: 09.00-16.00 (by appointment); Tube: Bromley-by-Bow.

Matt's Gallery E3

42-44 Copperfield Road   0181-983 1771   1–2D
This contemporary gallery commissions works, generally of an installation nature, which are made in, and specifically for, the space. / Times: Wed-Sun 12.00-18.00 (exhibitions only); Tube: Mile End.

North Woolwich Old Station Museum E16

Pier Road, North Woolwich   0171-474 7244   off map
This restored Victorian railway station, now a museum, tells the story of the local railways of east London and their impact on the areas they served. There are tickets, timetables, posters, a reconstructed 1920s ticket office and, of course trains. The first Sunday of every month (Easter-Oct) is a "steam day". Occasionally, there are film shows and model railway days. Ring to confirm opening times. / Times: Mon-Wed & Sat 10.00-17.00, Sun & Bank hols 14.00-17.00; Tube: East Ham (then 101 bus), Stratford (then 69 bus), North Woolwich.

Ragged School Museum E3

46-48 Copperfield Road   0181-980 6405   1–2D
This museum of the history of the East End is housed in a Victorian canalside warehouse which, from 1895, formed part of the largest Ragged (free) school in London. Appropriately, education and the life and work of Dr Barnardo are given particular emphasis, and there is a recreated Victorian classroom (which is used by school groups for re-enacted Victorian lessons). During the school holidays, amusing activities are organised. / Times: Wed & Thu 10.00-17.00, first Sun of month 14.00-17.00; Tube: Mile End.

Royal London Hospital Archives E1

St Augustine with St Philip's Church
Newark Street   0171-377 7000 x 3364   1–2D
A changing display, drawn from the many artefacts and archives which been accumulated over more than two centuries by the East End's best known hospital. While you're on the premises, it's worth viewing the very fine church (now a medical library) and the statue of Queen Alexandra (the only one in the country). There is also a statue of Edith Cavell, the first world war heroine and pioneer of modern nursing in Belgium, who did her training here. / Times: Mon-Fri 10.00-16.30; Tube: Whitechapel.

Spitalfields Market E1

Brushfield Street   0171-247 6590   5–2D
The City's former fruit and vegetable market (vacated in 1991), now owned by the same people as Camden Lock, has been transformed into a more general market, with stalls selling arts and crafts items and bric-à-brac, as well as an "international food hall". The large, covered area is becoming quite a popular place for a Sunday stroll. There are periodically special events, such as an Alternative Fashion Week. / Times: Mon-Fri 09.00-18.00, Sun 09.00-15.00; Tube: Liverpool Street.

The East End

The Showroom E2
44 Bonner Road   0181-983 4115   1–2D
Like at the other two galleries nearby (Matt's and the Chisenhale), the contemporary works displayed here are often installation-based. However, performance art (ie art involving people) is also an important part of the programme. / Times: Wed-Sun 13.00-18.00 (exhibitions only); Tube: Bethnal Green.

Valence House Museum, Essex
Becontree Avenue, Dagenham   0181-595 8404   off map
This partly-moated (mainly seventeenth century) manor house contains various artefacts, from the Stone Age onwards, which have been found locally. It's most notable contents, perhaps, are some fine portraits of the Fanshawe family, including those by Lely and Kneller. There are also displays of domestic interiors from the seventeenth and twentieth centuries and a walled herb garden. Children's workshops are held periodically. / Times: Tue-Fri 09.30-13.00, 14.00-16.30, Sat 10.00-16.00; Brit Rail: Chadwell Heath.

Vestry House Museum E17
Vestry Road   0181-509 1917   off map
This prettily situated former workhouse (1730) and police station was converted into a museum of local history in the 1930s. It is situated in the old village of Walthamstow, which is worth a view in its own right. The most singular exhibit is probably the Bremer Car – the first motor car to be made in London, by local engineer Frederick Bremer between 1892 and 1894. An original police cell (1840) is another curiosity. / Times: Mon-Sat 10.00-13.00, 14.00-17.30 (Sat 17.00).; Tube: Walthamstow Central.

West Ham United E13
Green Street, Upton Park   0181-548 2707   off map
The 'Hammers' are the only London club who open up for regular free open-days. If you would like to go 'back-stage' at The Boleyn Ground, then during the season on the first Thursday of each month they have tours at 10.00 and 14.00. / Tube: Upton Park.

Whitechapel Art Gallery E1
80 Whitechapel High Street   0171-522 7888   5–2D
This important non-commercial gallery, in its atmospheric, purpose-built Edwardian building, has no permanent collection. They therefore make a virtue of necessity by presenting an ever-changing series of exhibitions of twentieth century and contemporary art, often of important and challenging artists – for details call the recorded information line (tel 0171-522 7878). There is a programme of talks around the exhibitions, and sometimes also early evening films. / Times: Tue-Sun 11.00-17.00, Weds 11.00-20.00; Tube: Aldgate East.

William Morris Gallery E17

Lloyd Park, Forest Road   0181-527 3782   off map

William Morris, born in Walthamstow in 1834, was probably the most influential designer and craftsman London has ever produced. He died in 1896, but his ideas were carried on by the Arts and Crafts movement into the 1920s, and many of his designs, especially for wallpaper, are still in production today. This delightful eighteenth century house in its own grounds contains a display – completely re-designed not so long ago – of Morris's work and personal memorabilia, together with examples of the products of his associates Burne-Jones, Rossetti and Philip Webb. / Times: *Tue-Sat & first Sun of month 10.00-13.00, 14.00-17.00;* Tube: *Walthamstow Central.*

Outdoor attractions

Brick Lane E1, E2

1–2D

Forget the papers – roll up at 6 o'clock in the morning, or a little after if you must, to start off Sunday with a a truly East End "pile it high, sell it cheap" experience – "it" might be anything from food or toiletries to clothes and junk. / Times: *Sun 06.00-13.00;* Tube: *Aldgate, Aldgate East, Liverpool Street, Shoreditch.*

Canary Wharf E14

1–2D

Cesar Pelli's great tower (244 m high) on the Isle of Dogs is, at 50 stories, the second highest building in Europe. You don't actually need to approach very close to appreciate it – you can see it from points all over London – but if you do, there's an impressive shopping mall at its base, which, after a slow start, is beginning to have more life about it. The other shiny, new buildings around the tower's base, and the public spaces, are also worth a view. In Cabot Square, there is a rather unusual fountain controlled, via computer, by the speed and direction of the wind. The whole area is becoming more accessible, with the DLR now providing an all-day service, and, from spring 1995, at weekends as well. / Tube: *Canary Wharf (DLR).*

East Ham Nature Reserve E6

Norman Road, East Ham   0181-470 4525   off map

This suburban nature trail, set in London's largest churchyard, has the mission of introducing everyone to the joys of nature – the trail is fully accessible to all, including those in wheelchairs, and there is a guide available in Braille (from the visitor centre). Ring to ensure that the reserve is open before setting off. / Times: *Mon-Fri 09.00-17.00, Sat & Sun 14.00-17.00;* Tube: *East Ham.*

The mobile phone • For everyday • For everyone

Epping Forest, Essex

0181-508 0028   off map

*Twelve miles by two, this ancient forest on the eastern fringe of
London (owned by the Corporation of London since Victorian times)
is the largest open space in Essex. Much effort is put into
maintaining the landscape, with its diverse natural history, and over
three quarters of the area is designated as a Site of Special Scientific
Interest. Although, naturally, the forest is a very popular destination,
it's big enough that you can lose yourself in it – real countryside AND
accessible from an Underground station! A particular attraction is
Queen Elizabeth's Hunting Lodge (charge to visit), near Chingford,
which is the only surviving Tudor 'hunt-standing' (from which the
monarch could view the hunt's progress). There is an information
centre at High Beech, a popular spot about two miles from
Loughton, which organises occasional walks through the forest
(details from the number given).* / Times: *Information centre: 10.00
(Sun 11.00)-17.00 (summer); Mon-Fri 14.00-dusk, Sat 10.00-dusk,
Sun 11.00-17.00 (winter);* Tube: *Epping, Seydon Bois, Loughton, Snaresbrook.*

Greenwich Foot Tunnel E14

1–3D

See entry in the South section.

/ Times: *Lift service – Mon-Sat 08.30-19.00, Sun 10.00-17.30;*
Brit Rail: *Greenwich, Island Gardens (DLR).*

Hackney City Farm E2

1a Goldsmith's Row   0171-729 6381   1–2D

*Hackney City Farm keeps as full a range as possible of traditional
farm livestock in its 1 1/2 acre site. They also keep bees, and are
proud of their prize-winning herd of pedigree Saddle-back pigs.*

/ Times: *Tue-Sun 10.00-16.30;* Tube: *Bethnal Green.*

Lee Valley

Enquiries to: Countryside Centre, Abbey Gardens, Waltham
Abbey, Essex EN9 1XQ   01992 713838

*Since 1967, the then derelict valley of the River Lee has been being
transformed into a "green chain", extending all the way out from
Hackney, via Tottenham and Enfield, to the more truly rural delights
of Hertfordshire and Essex. If you wish, you can walk the whole 23
miles on the tow-path. It's still something of a patchwork at the
moment, but there's already a great variety of things to see and do
there, with attractions both natural (the variety of bird life and the
dragonfly sanctuary being particular features) and man-made
(including some pretty and historic buildings). If you're planning a
visit, the best course is to get in touch with the Countryside Centre,
which has a wide variety of leaflets detailing different aspects of the
park.* / Times: *Centre: 10.00-17.00 (Easter-Sep); Tue-Sun 10.30-16.30
(Oct-Easter);* Tube: *Tottenham Hale, or BR stations on L'pool St to Cambridge line.*

Mudchute Park and Farm E14
Pier Street   0171-515 5901   1–3D

The largest urban farm in the country, this 32 acre site is the most significant open space on the Isle of Dogs and includes a riding arena, fields, a wild section and a picnic area. Thousands of trees have recently been planted, and, as they develop, this place should become a real oasis. As it's several times bigger than most of the other farms, it can be run largely as if it were a small farm in the country, with its own grassland for grazing. On the livestock front, the speciality here is sheep, of which a wide variety are kept, but there are also cattle, goats and pigs, and they even have their own agricultural show, which is held during August. The park is becoming a popular attraction, and there is a café. / Times: *09.00-17.00;* Tube: *Crossharbour (DLR), Mudchute (DLR).*

Newham City Farm E16
King George Avenue   0171-476 1170   off map

This 4 1/2 acre farm has a wide range of livestock, including a shire horse, a donkey, cows, pigs, sheep, goats, chickens, ducks and geese. They are well geared up for casual visitors – 50,000 people pass through the gates each year – and, after a recent expansion into the neighbouring King George V park, they now have a visitors centre. / Times: *Tue-Sun 10.00-17.00 (16.00, winter);* Tube: *Prince Regent, Royal Albert (both DLR).*

Petticoat Lane E1
Certainly the best-known market in the East End, and possibly in the whole of London, the Sunday morning market here is a phenomenon worth seeing – whether or not your have any desire to buy some of the low-cost clothes for which the market is best known. / Times: *Sun 09.00-14.00;* Tube: *Liverpool Street, Fenchurch Street.*

Riverside Walks
See the South section for suggestions of interesting walks by the Thames.

St Katharine's Dock E1
1–2D

St Katharine's by the Tower (as the area is more properly called) is a fine collection of buildings, principally designed by the great nineteenth century engineer Thomas Telford, which have been restored to make a very attractive marina. It offers by far the nicest place for a riverside stroll in central London – the Tower of London and Tower Bridge providing a dramatic backdrop. In the summer, there is lunchtime music several times a week. / Tube: *Tower Hill.*

Spitalfields Community Farm E1
Weaver Street   0171-247 8762   1–2D

It may only have a site of 1 1/2 acre site of former waste-ground, but theu squeeze in most of the usual farm animals. / Times: *Tue-Sun 09.00-17.00 (winter),10.00-18.00 (summer);* Tube: *Shoreditch.*

Stepney Stepping Stones Farm E1

Stepney Way   0171-790 8204   1–2D

This 6 acre farm has all the main types of farm animals – cows, pigs, donkeys, sheep, goats, chickens, ducks, geese, rabbits and guinea pigs. There is also a picnic garden and a small library of books relating to farming. The venture, which has now been in existence for 15 years, is run entirely by volunteers and trainees, and partly funded by the sale of produce and home cooking. / Times: Tue-Sun 09.00-18.00; Tube: Stepney Green.

Tower Hamlets Cemetery Park E3

Southern Grove   0181-980 2373   1–2D

Built as a model necropolis for wealthy Londoners in 1841, this 27 acre site was used for burials until 1966. A period of neglect followed, during which the local flora and fauna established themselves with a vengeance, and in 1986 Tower Hamlets decided to make a virtue of necessity and declared the place a nature reserve. Some very fine Victorian tombs remain, and there is also a tree trail, which takes about 45 minutes to complete. / Times: 08.30-dusk; Tube: Mile End.

Victoria Park E3

Old Ford Road   0181-985 1957/6186   1–1D

In the 1840s, concern grew in east London about the lack of any recreation space for the burgeoning population. Fearing unrest, the government sold York House in Westminster to pay for the establishment of the new Victoria Park (of 220 acres), which is still the only large, formal park in the East End. Its style is very much in keeping with its name – it has lakes and fountains, large areas of bedding plants, a bandstand and a herd of fallow deer. Recent years have seen much refurbishment of the facilities. The oldest model boat club in the world meets here most Sunday mornings during summer. The emergency services use the park for their "999 Spectacular", usually in June. / Times: 07.30-dusk; Tube: Bethnal Green, Mile End.

West Ham Park E7

Upton Lane   0181-472 3584   off map

This 77 acre park in West Ham has been owned and run by the City Corporation since 1874. It boasts a number of recreational facilities, including a large children's playground, a keep fit trail and a 7 acre formal garden in the south east corner of the park. During the summer, there are children's entertainers at the bandstand, and, on Sunday afternoons, concerts. / Times: 07.30-30 mins before dusk; Tube: Plaistow.

Maps

Map I – Overview

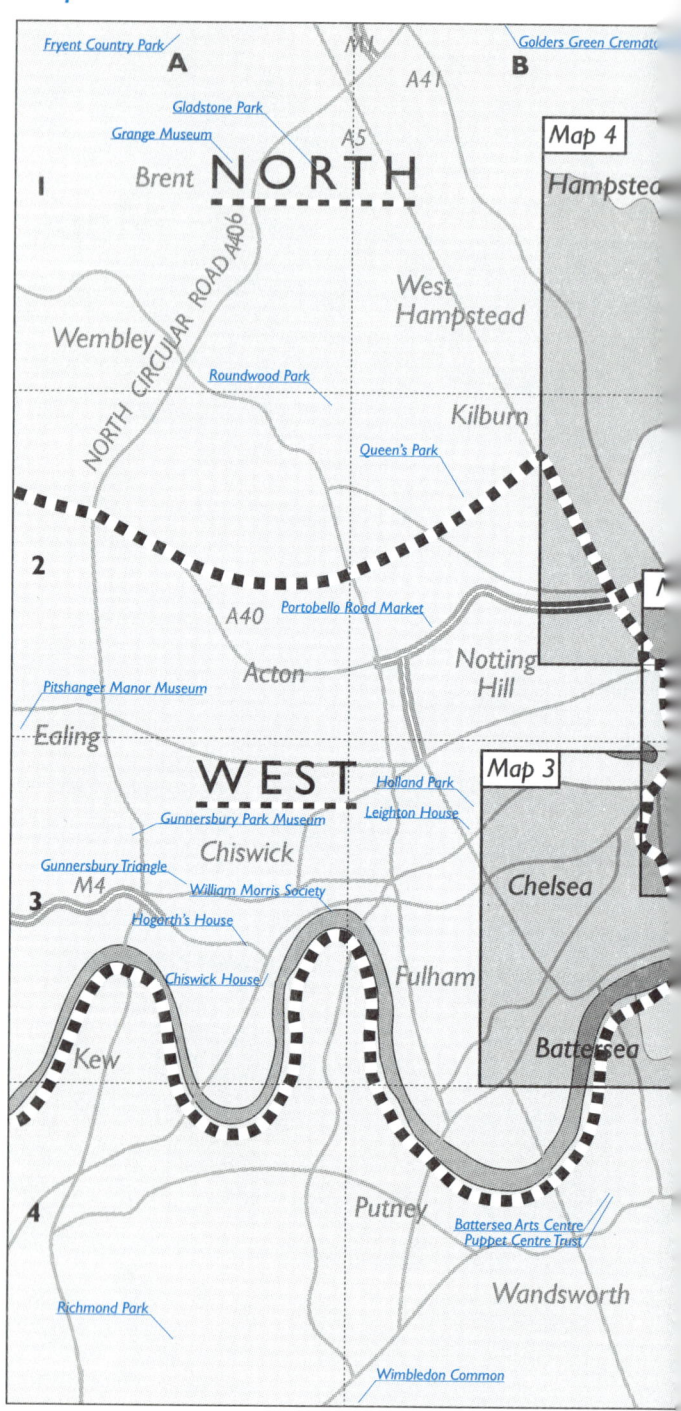

Fryent Country Park **A** M1 Golders Green Cremato

A41

Map 4

Gladstone Park

Grange Museum A5 **B**

Brent **NORTH** Hampstea

I

West
Hampstead

Wembley

NORTH CIRCULAR ROAD A406

Roundwood Park Kilburn

Queen's Park

2

A40

Portobello Road Market

Acton Notting
Hill

Pitshanger Manor Museum

Ealing

WEST

Holland Park **Map 3**

Gunnersbury Park Museum Leighton House

Gunnersbury Triangle Chiswick Chelsea

M4 William Morris Society

3

Hogarth's House

Chiswick House Fulham

Kew Battersea

4

Putney

Battersea Arts Centre
Puppet Centre Trust

Wandsworth

Richmond Park

Wimbledon Common

Map 1 – Overview

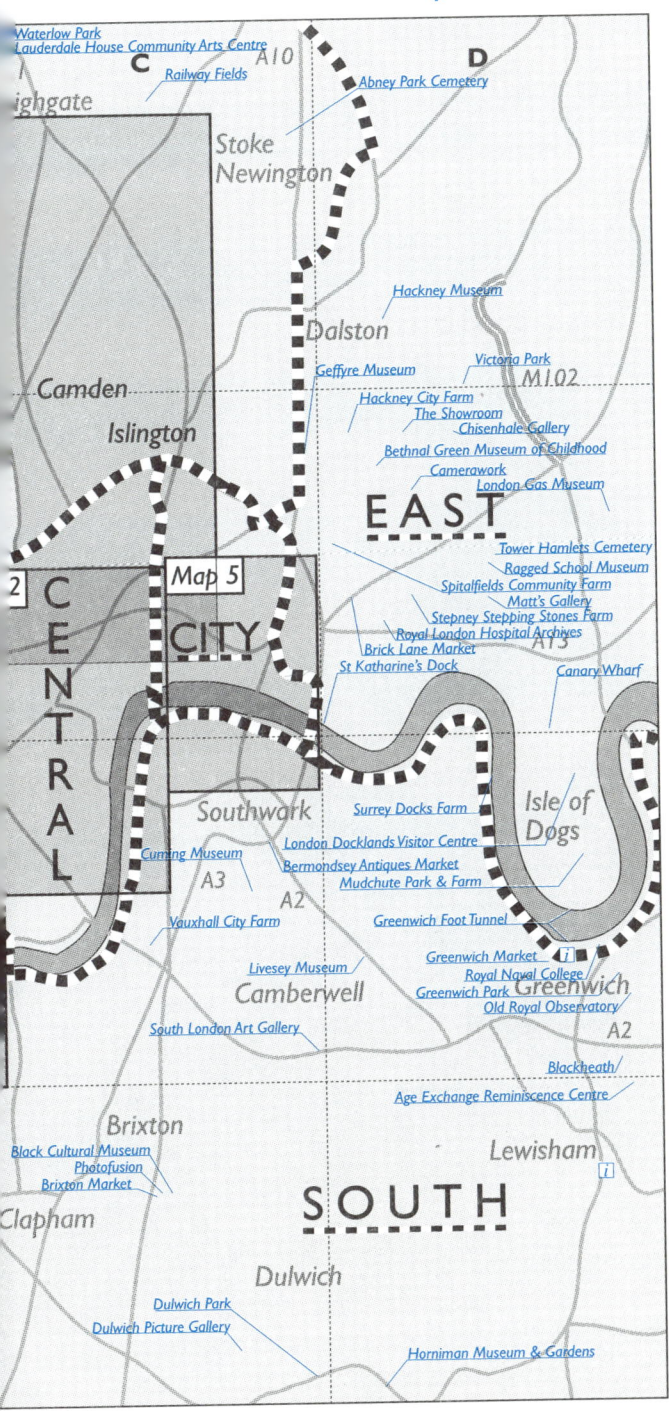

Map 2 – Central

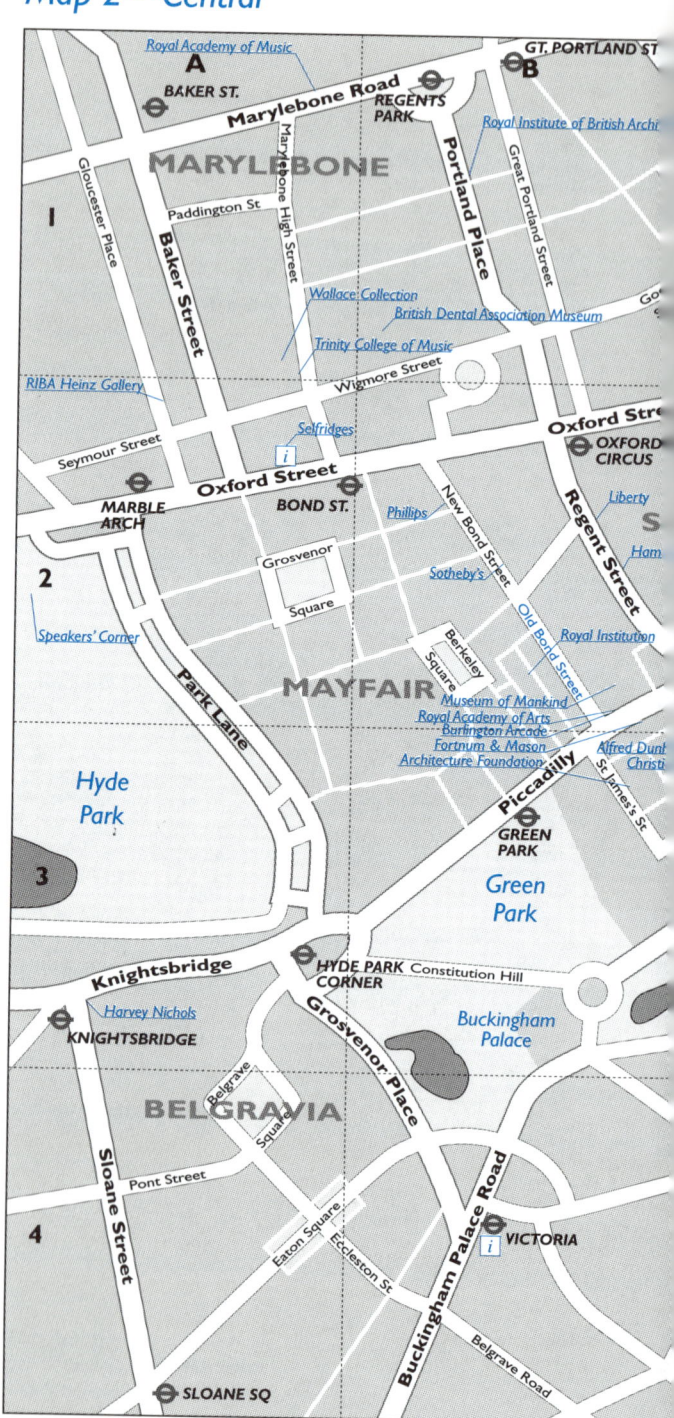

Map 2 – Central

Map 3 – West (SW postcodes)

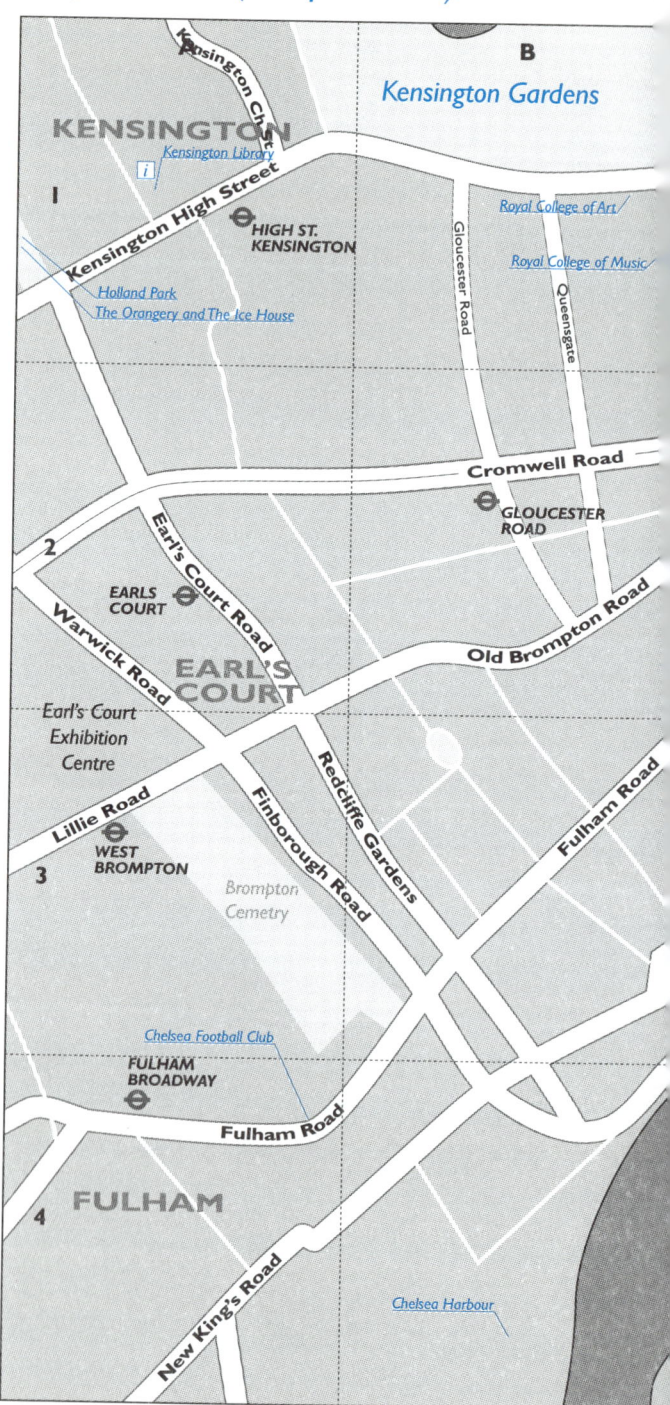

Map 3 – West (SW postcodes)

Map 4 – North

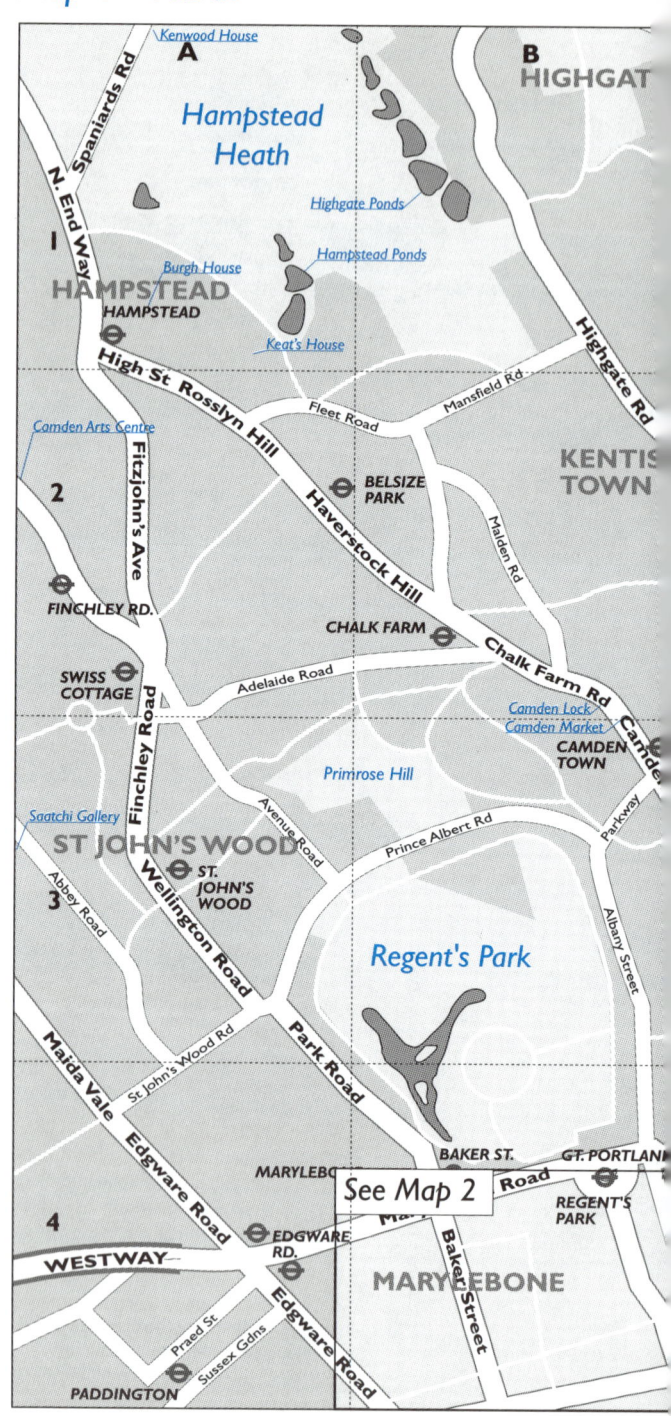

Kenwood House

A

B

HIGHGAT

Hampstead Heath

Highgate Ponds

Spaniards Rd

N. End Way

I

Burgh House

Hampstead Ponds

HAMPSTEAD

HAMPSTEAD

Keat's House

High St Rosslyn Hill

Fleet Road

Mansfield Rd

Highgate Rd

Camden Arts Centre

KENTIS
TOWN

2

Fitzjohn's Ave

BELSIZE
PARK

Haverstock Hill

Malden Rd

FINCHLEY RD.

CHALK FARM

Chalk Farm Rd

SWISS
COTTAGE

Adelaide Road

Camden Lock
Camden Market

Camde

Finchley Road

CAMDEN
TOWN

Saatchi Gallery

Primrose Hill

ST JOHN'S WOOD

Avenue Road

Prince Albert Rd

Parkway

Abbey Road

3

ST.
JOHN'S
WOOD

Albany Street

Wellington Road

Regent's Park

Maida Vale

Park Road

St John's Wood Rd

BAKER ST.

GT. PORTLAN

MARYLEBO

Road

Edgware Road

See Map 2

REGENT'S
PARK

4

WESTWAY

EDGWARE
RD.

Baker Street

MARYLEBONE

Edgware Road

Praed St

Sussex Gdns

PADDINGTON

Map 4 – North

C

FINSBURY PARK

Finsbury Park

FINSBURY PARK

Hornsey Road

Seven Sisters Rd

Blackstock Rd

ARSENAL

HWAY

TUFNELL PARK

Parkhurst Rd

HOLLOWAY RD.

Holloway Road

HIGHBURY AND ISLINGTON

Highbury Park

Brecknock Rd

KENTISH TOWN

Camden Road

CALEDONIAN RD.

Freightliners Farm

Union Chapel

Islington Museum Gallery

Liverpool Road

Upper Street

DEN RD

York Way

Caledonian Road

CAMDEN TOWN

ISLINGTON

Glasshouse

Essex Road

St Pancras Way

Camley Street Natural Park

MORNINGTON CRESCENT

Natural Museum of Cartoon Art

Pancras Rd

KING'S CROSS

Crafts Council

ANGEL

i

Eversholt Street

Hampstead Rd

EUSTON

Euston Road

Salvation Army Heritage Centre

Pentonville Road

City Road

Gray's Inn Rd

Farringdon Rd

Wellcome Building

ARREN ST.

EUSTON SQ.

BLOOMSBURY

Tottenham Court Rd

RUSSELL SQ.

Theobald's Rd

FARRINGDON

ODGE ST.

CHANCERY LANE

High Holborn

HOLBORN

TOTTENHAM COURT ROAD

Oxford Street

OXFORD CIRCUS

Fleet St

Map 5 – The City

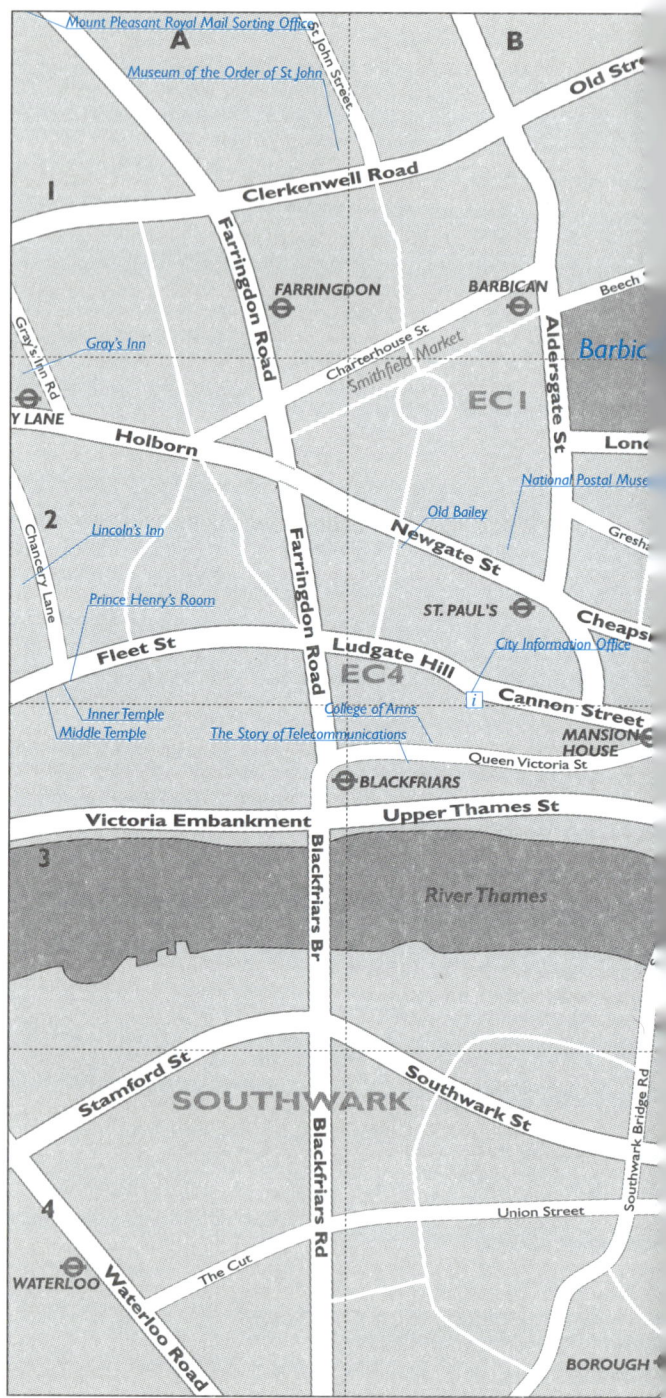

Mount Pleasant Royal Mail Sorting Office

Museum of the Order of St John

St John Street

B

Old Str

A

Clerkenwell Road

I

Farringdon Road

FARRINGDON

BARBICAN

Beech

Aldersgate St

Barbic

Gray's Inn

Gray's Inn Rd

Charterhouse St

Smithfield Market

EC1

Lond

Y LANE

Holborn

National Postal Muse

Chancery Lane

2

Lincoln's Inn

Old Bailey

Newgate St

Gresha

Farringdon Road

ST. PAUL'S

Cheaps

Prince Henry's Room

City Information Office

Fleet St

Ludgate Hill

EC4

Cannon Street

MANSION HOUSE

Inner Temple

Middle Temple

College of Arms

The Story of Telecommunications

Queen Victoria St

BLACKFRIARS

Victoria Embankment

Upper Thames St

Blackfriars Br

3

River Thames

Stamford St

SOUTHWARK

Southwark St

Southwark Bridge Rd

Blackfriars Rd

4

WATERLOO

Waterloo Road

The Cut

Union Street

BOROUGH

Map 5 – The City

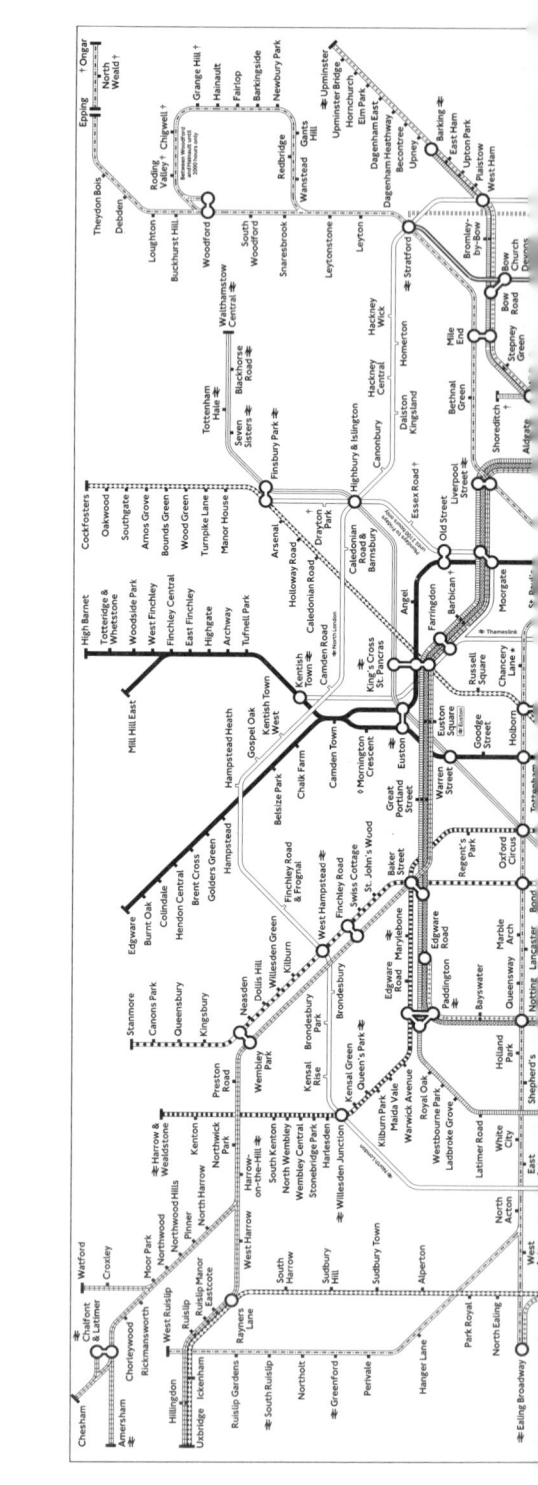

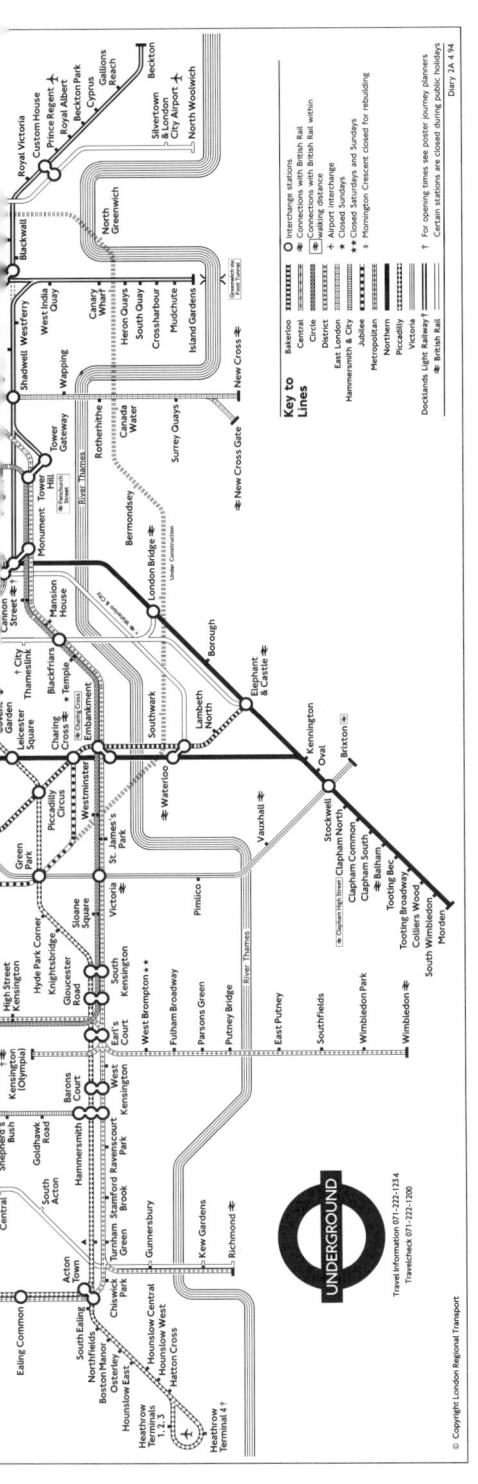

UNDERGROUND

Travel Information 071-222-1234
Travelchecks 071-222-1200

© Copyright London Regional Transport

Key to Lines

Bakerloo
Central
Circle
District
East London
Hammersmith & City
Jubilee
Metropolitan
Northern
Piccadilly
Victoria
Docklands Light Railway †
British Rail

○ Interchange stations
⊛ Connections with British Rail
⊞ Connections with British Rail within walking distance
✈ Airport interchange
★ Closed Saturdays and Sundays
★★ Closed Sundays
◇ Mornington Crescent closed for rebuilding

† For opening times see poster journey planners
‡ Certain stations are closed during public holidays

Diary 2A 4 94

Index

Parks and green spaces